Swisstory

The Untold, Bloody, and Absolutely Real History of Switzerland

By Laurie Theurer

Illustrated by Michael Meister

Bergli

For Gerd, Marlow and Savannah...
my favorite Swisstory.

–LT

For my (and all the other kids) who will create
our future's history

–MM

Swisstory: The Untold, Bloody, and Absolutely Real History
of Switzerland

English Edition: ISBN 978-3-03869-082-5 (Printed in the Czech Republic)
German Edition: ISBN 978-3-03869-083-2 (Printed in the Czech Republic)
Also available as an ebook

Bergli Books received a structural grant from the
Swiss Ministry of Culture 2016–2020

Table of contents

Swisstory

From the Cave

Needs good talisman

Winter inside

Winter outside

Not a pet

Fur

Brings trouble

Was a pet (was good stuff, too!)

Hot flame
(essential for
survival)

Prehistoric Swiss

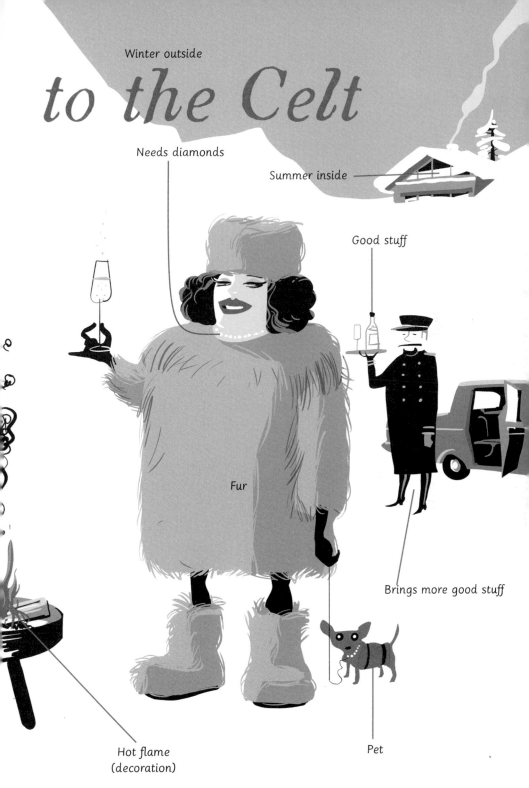

Winter outside

to the Celt

Needs diamonds

Summer inside

Good stuff

Fur

Brings more good stuff

Hot flame
(decoration)

Pet

Modern Swiss

From 120,000 to 10,000 BCE—give or take a few weeks—
Switzerland was covered in glaciers, which are thick layers of ice
and snow. In Lucerne, in fact, the ice is estimated to have been
about one kilometer thick...a real bummer for anyone who wanted
to take a boat ride on Lake Lucerne.

Lucerne in summer 88,000 BCE

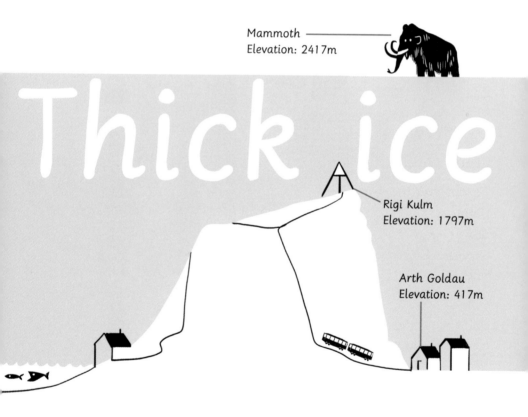

Mammoth
Elevation: 2417m

Rigi Kulm
Elevation: 1797m

Arth Goldau
Elevation: 417m

And it was cold. Really, really cold. Most people and animals
had migrated to warmer climates, but a few stuck around.
There were two types of cavemen (and cavewomen, of course)
before about 15,000 BCE—the Neanderthals and the Cro-Magnon.
Both evolved to survive in the harsh climate, but apparently the
Cro-Magnons were more successful at it because the others died out.

Cro-Magnon displaying superior reasoning skills

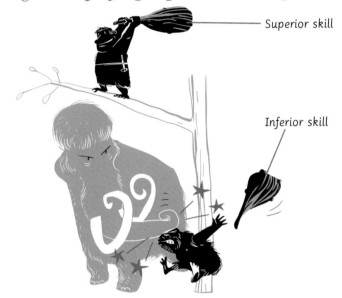

Superior skill

Inferior skill

Starting at about 20,000 BCE, temperatures in Europe started to rise and the area now known as Switzerland warmed up. Immense forests grew and the melting glaciers provided tons of lakefront property. The Lake Dwellers (called *Lacustrians*) built wooden houses high up on posts that they sank into the ground, just in case water levels rose.

Lacustrian real estate agents

It was built a few years ago by a nice couple. Unfortunately, they never learned to swim.

FOR SALE

The Lacustrians farmed the land; kept cattle, sheep, and pigs; but also hunted, fished, and gathered wild fruit and herbs...most likely in nearby woodlands where the land wasn't submerged.

These people were highly skilled. They made tools out of wood and stone, shoes and clothes out of tree bark, and worked with various metals—most notably copper and bronze.

Between 200 BCE and 100 BCE, various Celtic tribes—among them the Helvetians—made their way into Switzerland. The Celts were skilled at metalwork and could process iron to create super strong spears and swords that were much more durable than the bronze ones being made by everyone else.

Some historians maintain that the Celtic chariots were even superior to those of the Greeks and Romans.

Wheel envy

In fact, the Romans had fabulous chariots, but they used them for ceremonies, not war. So they were big, heavy, and not made for tight maneuvers. The Celts, on the other hand, created their chariots for warfare; they were smaller and lighter, made of wicker and wood, with sturdy iron-rimmed wheels. Even the famous Roman statesman Julius Caesar was jealous of them.

Around 200 BCE, the Romans, who were rapidly expanding their empire, decided that they wanted to add many parts of Switzerland to their territory. Led by Julius Caesar, the Romans quickly defeated the Helvetians and took over the land for about the next 150 years.

The Romans built cities, created a vast network of roads, and brought certain luxuries with them, all the while criticizing the Helvetians as "barbaric."

But who was more barbaric?

Helvetians	Romans

Hair stiff with chalked water

Silky locks

Real six-pack

Metal six-pack

Drank wine without diluting

Diluted wine with water

Screamed battle cries

No screaming while murdering

Equal social status, no castes

Nothing but castes

The Romans weren't all bad, though. They also introduced baths, floor heating, pottery, glass, tiles, bricks, plumbing, nails, cats, and garlic to the Helvetians. What would we do without those things today?

The Romans (or the Helvetians themselves under Roman rule) also established most of the largest Swiss cities still existing today, including Zurich (*Turicum*), Basel (*Basilia*), Lausanne (*Lousonna*), and Geneva (*Genava*). Clearly the Genevans were the only ones who remained almost fully satisfied with their Roman city name.

The Roman Empire came to an end during the 5th century, but it wasn't because of one lost battle or one dead king. There were lots of factors I won't go into here, but I will tell you about the very last stages.

Odoacer (433–493 CE)—a.k.a. Odovakar or Odovacar—was a German Barbarian who entered Italy in about 470 CE, joined the Roman army, and rose to a position of command. He overthrew the Roman general Orestes in 476 CE, sending him into hiding, and was proclaimed as the new Roman king by his troops.

Young Odoacer develops his very first five-year plan

Odoacer, where do you see yourself five years from now?

I'll have overthrown the school and pillaged neighboring communities by then.

Odoacer went on to launch attacks against his neighbors, conquering whatever new territory he could, until he met up with the Ostrogothic king Theodoric. This guy Theodoric did not mess around. Theodoric held a victory banquet in 493 CE and invited Odoacer, who was silly enough to show up. Theodoric killed him right in the middle of the second course.

Note: OK, we don't know exactly which course was being served when Odoacer was killed. Still...silly guy.

Dinner at Theodoric's house

MENU:

STARTER:
SOUP

MAIN COURSE:
ROAST DUCK
KILL ODOACER

DESSERT:
MELTED ICE
CREAM

The Barbarian Kingdoms (Franks, Alamanni, Vandals, Huns, Goths, and others) continued their power struggles within Europe until, by 534 CE, Switzerland found itself occupied by Burgundians and Franks in the west, and Alamanni in the east.

The Burgundians were originally from Denmark but ended up adopting the dialect of the people living in the western part of Switzerland (which eventually became French). The Alamanni used a language that eventually became German. Over the coming hundreds of years, the dividing line between the two languages and cultures became more and more noticeable. The division between the two eventually (ok, about 1000 years later) became known as the *Rösti ditch* (*Röstigraben* or *rideau de rösti*).

Rösti is a hashed potato dish eaten widely in the German-speaking part of Switzerland, but not usually eaten in the French part. But nobody could have seen this coming, as potatoes were not even introduced to Europe until they were first brought over from South America in the late 16th century.

Potato's arrival in Switzerland

Swiss-French potato vs. Swiss-German potatoes

Why it never came to be called the au gratin ditch, the world will never know.

Some people also claim there is a polenta ditch between both of these two regions and the Italian-speaking region in the south of Switzerland. Anything to be able to laugh at each other, right?

All for One, and One for All!
Unus pro omnibus, omnes pro uno
(the unofficial motto of Switzerland)

Blown Away *By*

Alphorn for beginners

Taaa = "Cows, come to me."

Taaa-taaa = "Hey, other shepherds, want to meet up for a beer? Bring beer."

The Alphorn

Taaa-taaa-taaa = "Gather round. It's time to go to war!"

Taaa-taaa-taaa-taaa = "Hi Mom, send up more toilet paper!"

So, what's the deal with the alphorn? Who invented it? What for? As the world's worst five-kilogram fashion accessory? Unlikely.

Over the centuries, the alphorn has been used for a variety of reasons. Since it can be heard five kilometers away, or more, cowherds would often use it to signal to other cowherds...kind of like a ginormous mobile phone. Cowherds also use it to call the cows in from the pasture at milking time, and some even play it while actually milking the cows. Apparently, it has a soothing effect that can stimulate milk production...for the cows. Not the cowherds.

Alphorn. Alpenhorn. Alpine Horn.
Whatever you choose to call it, there's no mistaking
this three-to-four-meter-long wooden horn that...

A: Looks like the world's biggest bubble blower
And, depending on who you ask, EITHER
B: Sounds like heaven on earth
OR
C: Sounds like a constipated cow

Horns have been used in wartime for centuries. Trumpets, bugles, and animal horns have called troops into battle in nearly every region of the world. Switzerland, too, roused troops with the use of horns. Not so much alphorns, though. Imagine lugging a three-meter-long horn into battle. By the time you took it out, put it together, got it into position, and started blowing, all your troops would be dead.

Nope, the alphorn is a very different type of horn from the others. Nobody knows exactly when or where—or why—it was first invented, but it was probably something roughly like this...

Prehistoric alphorn

We know that the alphorn was invented at the latest during the second century, as a 160 CE Roman mosaic featuring a shepherd with an alphorn has been found in Vaud, Switzerland. So far, that's our earliest finding of an alphorn to date—but there's still a lot we don't yet know about its earliest history.

The earliest known written mention of the alphorn is from 1527. Whoever kept the accounting book of the monastery of St. Urban wrote down, "Two coins for a Valaisan with Alphorn." This meant that somebody from Valais played his alphorn and the monastery accountant paid him for his playing.

Two coins for a Valaisan with alphorn

In the 15th and 16th centuries, we know that the Alphorn was often used as a source of income by off-season cowherds. Since the cows were housed in the barns during winter, there was no work for these men, and they found themselves a bit short on cash. So they set their horns up in the villages and performed for donations, earning themselves a bit of a bad reputation as beggars.

Then came John Calvin, a Frenchman with very rigid ideas about right and wrong. After being kicked out of France for his radical ideas, he found a home in Geneva in the 1540s, where his ideas took root and spread. Calvin believed, among other things, that instrumental music was the work of the devil. Unless it was church music…that was ok. So he ensured that instruments were destroyed and people were punished for playing most kinds of music. Eventually, alphorn playing was outlawed in the parts of Switzerland that followed Calvin's ideas. The alphorn very nearly disappeared forever.

Calvin meets the alphorn

Then came Napoleon, who invaded Switzerland in 1798 and stuck around for several years. During this time, the Swiss were deeply divided again, with vastly different ideas about whether or not French occupation was a good thing, what religion should be practiced, etc., etc., etc.

After Napoleon finally left Switzerland, the mayor of Bern had an idea he hoped would soothe the Swiss people and help them forget their deep differences and disagreements. He created a festival of Alpine Traditions—the Unspunnen Festival.

The Unspunnen Festival

Pin-the-tail on Napoleon

Whack-a-Napoleon

Kissing Booth

The festival was held in August 1805 near Interlaken. There were displays of regional dancing, singing, costumes and food, crossbow shooting, wrestling, boulder-throwing, as well as competitions in alphorn playing. An unbelievable three thousand people attended. Unfortunately, only two people showed up for the alphorn competition.

The alphorn competition was canceled and both contestants were sent home with a medal and a black sheep. In 1808, only one of the alphorn players showed up for the competition.

Low point for the alphorn

1805 in Unspunnen: Sepp and Urs

1808 in Unspunnen: Sepp

Enough was enough! The mayor of Bern decided that steps must be taken to save the alphorn from disappearing from Swiss culture forever. He hired an alphorn player—Ferdinand Fürchtegott Huber—(yes, his middle name means "god-fearing") who taught music at the Fellenberg Institute to train six people in the art of alphorn playing. The mayor had six new alphorns made and arranged for Huber to take six students up to the mountains during the summer each year to learn how to play them. This action most likely saved the alphorn from extinction. It took some years and more than a bit of money to make the alphorn the national icon it is today, but eventually the charm of the alphorn spread again throughout Switzerland. It was (and is) promoted as a symbol of Swiss culture and has become a valuable tourist attraction. One of the longest instruments in the world—that coincidentally plays one of the fewest amounts of notes—is here to stay.

Castle (or château, mansion, palace)

The Hideous Habsburgs

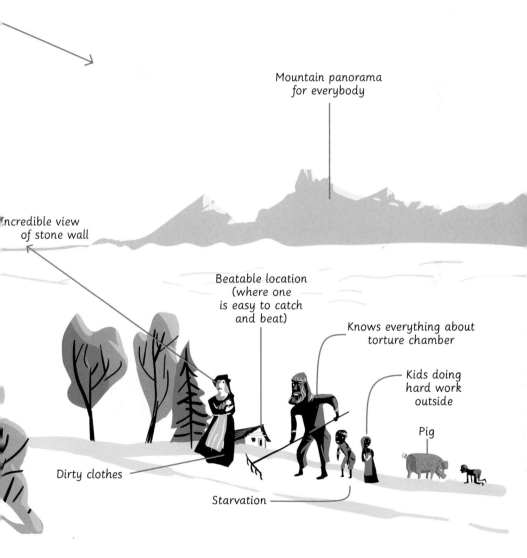

Mountain panorama
for everybody

Incredible view
of stone wall

Beatable location
(where one
is easy to catch
and beat)

Knows everything about
torture chamber

Kids doing
hard work
outside

Pig

Dirty clothes

Starvation

House (or cottage, shack, hovel)

If you've seen a castle still standing in Switzerland, chances are good that it was built by one of the Habsburgs.

"So, who were the Habsburgs?" you ask. Good question.

The Habsburgs were one of the most powerful families in Europe between the 1400s and 1800s. They had lands and servants, titles and crowns, as well as most of Europe bowing down before them. They were counts, dukes, kings, and even emperors of the Holy Roman Empire (HRE). So, in other words, they had lots of goodies. Not too shabby, eh? But it sure sucked for the rest of the people—the ones without the goodies.

Before the Habsburgs took things over, Switzerland was not yet Switzerland. Instead it was simply a bunch of people living in towns, villages, or out in the middle of nowhere, answering to whatever local medieval family had power at the time. Life overall was not too terrible, especially if you didn't mind squalor and smells and stuff like that, but people were more or less free to live it.

Quality of life in medieval times

Peasant home life

Peasants on vacation

Enter the horrible Habsburgs

Count Radbot (985-1045 AD)

It all started with Count Radbot of Swabia, a.k.a. "The Founder." This guy wasn't really so horrible, but he was important. Without him, there would have been no Habsburgs. And without the Habsburgs, there would have been no Switzerland.

Aside from having a goofy name, Count Radbot belonged to a relatively unknown German family living in what is now Aargau, Switzerland. He built a beautiful Benedictine abbey in Muri and, between 1020 and 1030 CE, got it into his head to build a small castle in Aargau. He called it "Habichtsburg" (Hawk Castle), supposedly after seeing a hawk sitting on its walls one fine day. A few generations later, the name "Habichtsburg" had morphed into "Habsburg," and Radbot's descendants, who had become really rich and powerful, adopted the name as their own.

Timing is everything. What if, on that fine day, instead of gazing at a hawk, Radbot had seen a wild pig scratching its butt against the wall?

The family name might have been very different

By then, most of Europe—including what is now called Switzerland—belonged to the Holy Roman Empire. The pre-Swiss lands were sitting there, looking like a yummy, juicy pie... and the greedy Habsburg family wanted a huge slice. The problem with having lots of goodies is that it makes you want to have even more goodies...doesn't it? It's like with potato chips. You can't eat just one. You have to keep eating until you're ready to barf.

That's how it went for the Habsburgs, too

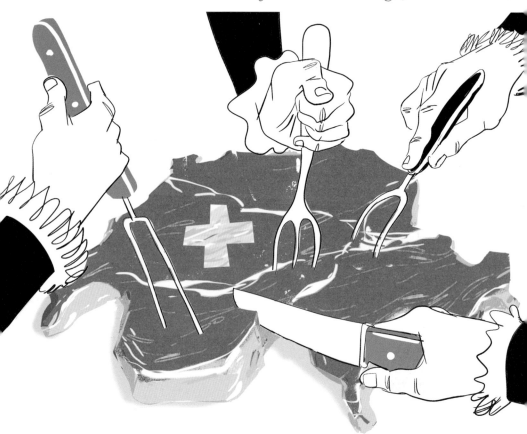

Radbot's descendants, it seems, were greedier and crueler than their founder in their quest for more. As their territory within Switzerland grew, so did their viciousness.

The modern Swiss have plenty of stories about their oppression by the Habsburg dynasty, as well as how they fought back, particularly against the governors who controlled particular regions. Some are true, and some are the stuff of myth and legend, but every one of them shaped the future of Switzerland and made it what it is today.

Arnold of Melchtal versus the Habsburg Landenberger

During the early 1300s, a bad-tempered Habsburg governor named Landenberger would often insult and demean an old and locally respected peasant named Heinrich of Melchtal. One day, Landenberger decided to accuse Heinrich of an offense that he hadn't committed. Heinrich's punishment was to hand over his team of oxen to one of Landenberger's messengers. When the old man complained he couldn't work his fields if he lost his oxen, the messenger told Heinrich that he should pull the plough himself instead, as he was only a lowly peasant. Heinrich's son, Arnold, heard this and fought back, attacking the messenger with a stick and breaking his fingers.

As a punishment, Landenberger confiscated Heinrich's small property, charged him a heavy fine, and had Heinrich's eyes burned out of his sockets with hot irons

It's not surprising that the local peasants grew to hate Landenberger so much that they decided to take matters into their own hands. On Christmas Eve 1308, while Landenberger was at church, forty of them showed up at his castle near Sarnen carrying gifts for the governor. When they were let in, they pulled out the weapons hidden in their clothing, attacked the guards, and took possession of the castle, eventually burning it to the ground.

Landenberger heard about the siege while still at church and ran away to Lucerne, no doubt labeled as a coward for the rest of his life

Conrad of Baumgarten versus the Habsburg Wolfenschiessen

Wolfenschiessen was a Habsburg bailiff with an eye for a peasant woman who was happily married to Conrad of Baumgarten. Wolfenschiessen (yes, that translates as "shooting the wolf"), tried to seduce Baumgarten's wife for the hundredth time while Baumgarten was away from the house. Wolfie entered the house without permission and ordered her to draw him a bath. The wife, apparently tired of Wolfie harassing her, decided to trick him instead. She drew a bath and told him that she would step into the other room to get undressed.

Wolfie hopped into the tub and waited. But...

She snuck out the window and ran to get her husband, who sped back to the house with axe in hand...

...and turned the bathtub into a pot of chopped Wolfie stew

True, the Habsburg tyrants were cruel. They were rich, powerful, and skilled at warfare. But they had met their match. Yes, the pre-Swiss were poor, geographically isolated from each other, disorganized, and they didn't have weapons or warfare skills. But they had a deep love of their land and their freedom. There was no question that the pre-Swiss would one day rise up and defy the tyrants. The Habsburgs never had a chance.

But in the end, it wasn't only the pre-Swiss who can take the credit for defeating the Habsburgs. Nope. The greedy Habsburgs also did it to themselves. Read on.

The Habsburg jaw

There's an old saying that goes like this: "Be careful what you wish for. It just might come true."

The Habsburgs wanted all the goodies for themselves, but keeping so much power in one family came at a cost that nobody could have imagined—especially not the Habsburgs.

Generation after generation of Habsburg degeneration

Something weird started showing up in the Habsburg family. Prepare yourself. It was a jaw. Not just a jaw, but a long, protruding lower jaw covered in drool—first appearing in Maxmilian I, born in the middle of the 15th century. Turns out that the Habsburg family, in their attempts to keep their riches in the family—and to get even more—had started marrying off their sons and daughters to other rich royal families. That would increase both family fortunes, right? Well, maybe. But what if the most desirable families to marry into are closely related to your own?

Well, that's exactly what the Habsburgs started doing... inbreeding. I know...*ick*, right? Let's just say that inbreeding is always a really, really bad idea.

A normal, healthy person has a mishmash of genes inherited from their parents, who are usually not closely related. In fact, the more the parents' genes differ from each other, the stronger and healthier their children are likely to be. If the parents' genes are too much alike, their children can suffer from a whole bunch of genetic problems.

Enter the Habsburgs. After more than sixteen generations of inbreeding, the Spanish line of the family completely wiped themselves out. The last Habsburg in the Spanish branch of the family was poor old Charles II (1661–1700), who should win the prize for the most confusing family tree ever. His father was his mother's uncle, his grandmother was also his aunt, and his great-grandmother was also his grandmother. If that's not confusing enough, all eight of his great-grandparents were direct descendants of the same people (Joanna and Philip I of Castile). In fact, Joanna of Castile appears fourteen times in Charles' family tree. And yes...double ick!

Now that's a genealogist's worst nightmare!

33

The result, of course, was that poor Charles II was born with a long list of genetic problems. He was short, weak, mentally handicapped, and had intestinal issues. His lower jaw was so sticky-outie that he couldn't speak until he was four years old. He was unable to walk until he was eight. He had trouble chewing due to his large tongue and he frequently drooled. He was also impotent and sterile, which meant no kids for Charles II. The Spanish ridiculed him, calling him "El Hechizado" (the Hexed One) until he died at the age of thirty-eight with no heirs. That was the end of the Habsburg line in Spain.

The Habsburg line in Austria—which ruled over Switzerland until the pre-Swiss kicked their butts out—continued somewhat longer than the one in Spain, long-jawed and drooling as it was. Family members continued to marry each other, and their children continued to suffer from it.

Triple ick!

Inbreeding didn't end the dynasty, though.
It was a curse that did it.

The curse of Countess Karolyi

As they say, all things good and evil must come to an end.

In 1848, after a group of Hungarians rebelled against Habsburg rule in their country, eighteen-year-old Emperor Franz Joseph had them all executed. One of the rebels was the son of Countess Karolyi of Hungary, who immediately placed a curse on the young Emperor and his family.

The curse

Some say that the tragedies which struck the Habsburg family from this point forward were of their own doing, as they were so power-hungry that they inbred themselves to the point of madness. Others say it was the curse. You can decide for yourself.

From the time of the curse, the horrible Habsburgs suffered like they had never suffered before.

For the next seventy years, or so, Habsburg family members...

Went bonkers

Committed suicide

Were shot by firing squad

Were lost at sea

Were accidentally burned alive

Died after falling off horses

PAW

Were murdered
by anarchists

In 1914, the murder of the Habsburg Franz Ferdinand triggered World War I and led to the dismantling of the entire Habsburg Empire.

Ironic, isn't it? The Habsburgs were so hungry to hold onto their power that, whether losing to the Swiss, starting an inbreeding program, or attracting curses, their ambition and greed eventually ended up destroying them. However, without all of this horribleness, Switzerland would not be what it is today—a free land, governed by its own people, full of really cool, old Habsburg castles to do with what we please.

Bacon Butt Castle
Address: 5245 Bacon Butt Village
General Contractor: Radbot, Count of Bacon Butt
Built: approximately 1030 CE
Function: Castle, fortification, status symbol, museum, butt-scratching post

William Tell

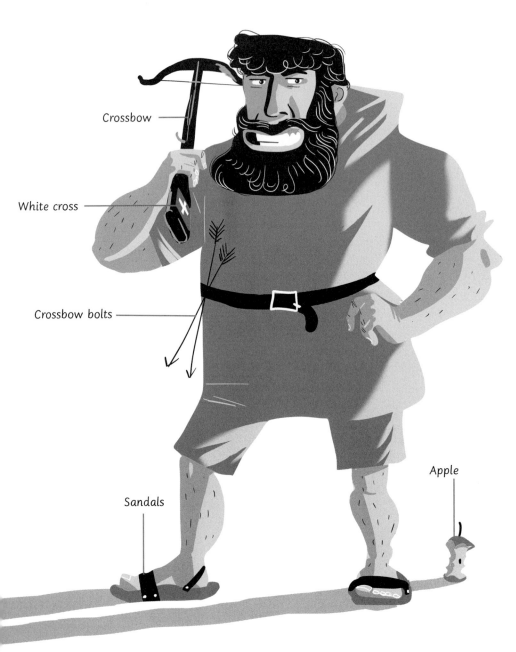

Crossbow

White cross

Crossbow bolts

Sandals

Apple

The legendary William Tell

The real William Tell

Have you heard the story of William Tell and the horrific Habsburg governor named Gessler? Let's see if this version sounds familiar to you...

William Tell was a peaceful man who lived in the small village of Bürglen, Switzerland during the 14th century.

Back then, the Switzerland we know now did not yet exist. Instead, the horrible Habsburg family of Austria were the emperors of the Holy Roman Empire, the self-proclaimed bosses of the lands, including what is now known as Switzerland—and they were not kind to its proud peasants.

So, the Habsburgs appointed a governor—the cruel and brutal (and possibly made up) Hermann Gessler—to rule from the nearby town of Altdorf. Gessler, for reasons only known to tyrants, ordered his men to do this...

Gessler had a pole placed in the central square of Altdorf and ordered that his own hat be stuck on top of it. The hat would represent Gessler, and every villager was supposed to pay respect to the hat…as if it were Gessler himself. According to this story, on November 18th, 1307, William Tell and his youngest son,

Walter, visited Altdorf to get some supplies. They walked through the town square…straight past the pole with Gessler's hat on it… without bowing! William Tell and little Walter were arrested and were forced to face the rage of the evil Governor Gessler.

An apple was found and Gessler issued his ultimatum. William Tell must either shoot the apple off his son's head, or both of them would rot in jail until the end of their days. William Tell bound his little son to the trunk of a tree and balanced the apple on top of his head.

William Tell pulled out two crossbow bolts, loaded one, and took aim at the fruit on his son's head. He shot straight through the apple on his first try and won their freedom.

William Tell was arrested and shackled...while apparently Walter was forgotten completely. He ran off to play with his friends, or to finish eating the apple. Nobody knows. Gessler's men discussed the best way to transport Tell to Gessler's dungeon.

And so they set off for Küssnacht by boat...about to shut William Tell away in a musty dungeon forever. Or were they?

So off they went. On the way to Küssnacht, Tell steered the boat up to a large, flat slab of rock, and then...

Tell managed to leap out, and then pushed the boat containing Gessler and his men back into the stormy lake.

In the meantime, William Tell ran through forests and fields all the way to Küssnacht, with Gessler and his men not far behind. William Tell found a place to hide on the Hohle Gasse near Gessler's castle...and waited. Oh yes, and somehow he got his crossbow and bolts back...

When Gessler appeared on the Hohle Gasse, Tell used his crossbow to shoot him straight through the heart before making his escape. Tell fled back to Bürglen and, as far as the story goes, was never bothered by Gessler's men again.

William Tell reportedly lived to quite an old age and had plenty of other adventures we won't go into here. According to legend, he died in 1354 while trying to save a drowning child in the Schächenbach River.

So he dove in and he was washed away down the raging river.

William Tell's body never washed up—neither in the river nor in the Lake of Lucerne. And this man, this symbol of Swiss resistance, remains a legend and a national hero to this day.

What muscle!
What courage!
What a beard!
What an unbelievable legend!!

WILLIAM TELL—THE GREATEST HERO THAT NEVER LIVED.

But here's the problem with my story. I probably never existed. I might even be an old Danish story everyone pretended happened in Switzerland. Walter, the apple, that famous crossbow shot: just one big lie.

But that doesn't mean that my legend wasn't important. When times are tough, people need a hero. Think about Robin Hood, Superman, and The Three Musketeers. None of these heroes were real, but all became popular in times of trouble when people desperately needed to find hope.

When my story came about, the people in the region now known as Switzerland were fed up. They'd been attacked on all sides for ages by other nations and dynasties that were trying to grab more land and wealth for themselves. The communities of Switzerland, especially the founding "forest cantons" of Uri, Schwyz, and Unterwalden, were already talking about making a pact to protect each other against outside powers. My story helped them. I showed them that it was possible to fight back, to resist, and to win. Which they did.

No wonder the Swiss people love my legend so fiercely. I'm awesome, even if I never existed.

The Rütli

Oath

According to legend, three Swiss men met on the Rütli meadow on the shores of Lake Lucerne in November of 1307. They came from the forest cantons of Uri, Schwyz, and Unterwalden, and pledged to support and protect each other against domination by the horrible Habsburgs, emperors of the Holy Roman Empire.

The Rütli Oath: *as they say it happened*

Well, that's how the legend goes, anyway. But legends, as we've seen, are sometimes true, sometimes partly true, and sometimes complete and utter nonsense. Historians don't agree on whether the Rütli Oath actually took place and—if they can't agree— how are we supposed to know?

Let's go back once again to the end of the 13th century. Duke Albrecht of Austria became the Habsburg Ruler and decided fairly quickly that the lands of Uri, Schwyz, and Unterwalden looked mighty good indeed. He sent two bailiffs to control the region and to force it under Habsburg rule...clearly without a clue how thoroughly the Swiss were about to kick Habsburg butt.

According to the legend

So, Gessler and Landenberg, time to go boss around some ignorant peasants. You ready?

You betcha! Time to squeeeeeze a lot of taxes out of those villagers.

I've already packed, Your Excellence, and I made sure to bring along my favorite hat.

According to the legend, too

Cow poo

When Gessler and Landenberg arrived in the heart of Switzerland, they found that the locals were not about to let themselves get pushed around. At least that's how the story goes when told by the Swiss themselves...

Werner Stauffacher was a wise and respected man living in Steinen, Schwyz. He was the elected judge and leader of his region and lived in a fine house built of stone.

And who are you to live in such a fine stone house?

I'm the judge and leader of this region, sir.

So, Stauffacher met with his friends, Walter Fürst—a wise and respected man from Uri—and Arnold von Melchtal—a wise and respected man from Unterwalden.

So, the three men pledged to meet again on the Rütli meadow during November 1307. It was a secret meeting, so of course they each brought at least ten of their friends. While at Rütli, the men vowed to defend each other against the horrible Habsburgs and anybody else who wanted to disrupt their way of life.

This moment is regarded by the Swiss as the founding moment of their country. It's been celebrated every year since its occurrence on August 1st, 1291…Switzerland's birthday.

But…wait a second! Didn't we just say that the secret meeting at the Rütli meadow was during November 1307? Why is Switzerland's birthday celebrated as August 1st, 1291?

That's sixteen years and three months before the Rütli Oath.

Since there is no historical record of the Rütli Oath, nobody can prove that it really happened...and historians disagree on whether it actually *did* happen.

The first mention of the Rütli Oath in writing appeared in *The White Book of Sarnen*, about 162 years after the oath supposedly took place. The book was written by Hans Schriber, the state secretary of Unterwalden in 1470. Trouble is, Schriber was copying information from earlier documents and those documents no longer exist. So, the details in *The White Book of Sarnen* could be perfectly true, or they could be total lies. Nobody will ever know. This means that many Swiss have come to rely on *The White Book of Sarnen*—and on a legend passed down orally through multiple generations—as fact.

If that wasn't already messed up enough, the next written information about the Rütli Oath was recorded by Aegidius Tschudi in his *Chronicon Helveticum* in 1550. Tschudi repeated the same Rütli Oath story as in *The White Book of Sarnen* but, truth be told, he was known to add all kinds of stuff that never really happened to his stories.

William Tell tells the truth

He also wrote about me in the Chronicon Helveticum as if I really existed, when most historians now agree that I probably didn't.

Wait. It gets more messed up.

As it turns out, the 1st of August 1291 doesn't have much to do with the Rütli Oath. It has more to do with the Federal Charter.

The Federal Charter is a document that describes the alliance between Uri, Schwyz, and Unterwalden—that alliance many people consider to be the beginning of Switzerland. Yep, the very same cantons that were supposedly involved in the Rütli Oath. Historians generally agree that the Federal Charter and the Rütli Oath probably didn't have much to do with each other. But— stay with me here—they also agree that Walter Fürst (from Uri), Werner Stauffacher (from Schwyz), and Arnold von Melchtal (from Unterwalden) were very likely the men behind the Federal Charter, as they were considered the political elite at that time. If something important happened, they would have been involved.

Federal Charter non-starter

So, were we involved in the Federal Charter or the Rütli Oath? Or both? Or neither?

Good question, guys. On a document of such historical importance involving three cantons, you would expect there to be at least three signatures, right? Even back then, the Swiss would have been very exact about such a thing.

But there are no signatures on the Federal Charter!

There's also no exact date, no mention of the place where it was created, as well as a whole bunch of spelling and grammatical errors. That's a whole bunch of sloppy for a very Swiss document.

But it gets weirder.

The Federal Charter was the most important document in Swiss history, about the most important event. But after it was made, it was stuck away in an archive in canton Schwyz... and pretty much ignored for 500 years. No one cared.

That sucks

Is it just us, or does that kind of suck?

The Federal Charter was discovered in 1758 in the archives of Canton Schwyz and was made use of again about 140 years later.

The Federal Charter suddenly becomes important

During the 19th century, much of Europe was going through a period of "enhanced nationalism." That means that national pride—and celebrations of national pride—were trending in most European countries. Nearly every European country had its own National Day…and the Swiss government desperately wanted one of its own.

So, in November 1889, the Federal Council ordered two governmental agencies to figure out how to create a Swiss National Day.

As it turned out, Bern was about to celebrate its 700-year anniversary in 1891 and the government wanted to combine the 600-year anniversary of Switzerland with that celebration. After all, the plans were already made for the Bern celebration. Two birds, one stone.

Sixteen days later, the two governmental agencies turned in their report. The government decided that the Swiss Confederation began on the 1st of August, as this was the date of the Federal Charter. Never mind that the Federal Charter doesn't actually contain an exact date. It just says something about being written at the start of August. No bother.

The date was perfect, the document was perfect…enough… and it would allow Switzerland to celebrate its first National Day already in 1891. If they had chosen the Rütli Oath date of November 1307, they would have had to wait until 1907 for their celebration…and celebrate in the November cold!

So that was that. Switzerland was suddenly founded on the 1st of August 1291, even though this date meant nothing whatsoever to most Swiss citizens at the time.

National Day celebrations on the 1st of August 1891

Since then, of course, the 1st of August 1291 has grown to mean a GREAT deal to the Swiss—regardless of which part of the country they come from or what language they speak. One cringe-worthy fact for you, though—most Swiss people don't quite understand *why* this day is celebrated.

A national magazine did a survey of the Swiss in 2016, asking random people on the street why their National Day is on the 1st of August. *Only 45% of those responding gave the right answer.* A whopping 33% gave the wrong answer and 22% said they had absolutely no idea. Lucky you. Now you can tell them.

Not quite a plume

Charmed

What he is fighting for:
his beloved Vreneli

Cow

Limited wooden protection

Cow poo (fly)

Deadly look

Swiss Guy

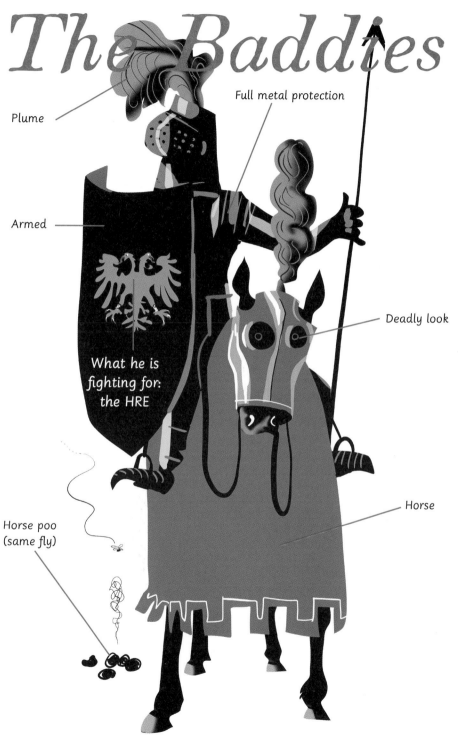

Since pretty much the beginning of time, the Swiss were surrounded by nasty, aggressive neighbors who wanted to take away their lands and freedoms. The Swiss had to either give up or defend themselves and their land.

We can choose our friends, but we can't choose our neighbors

11th century:
The House of Savoy

12th century:
The Zähringens

15th century:
The Burgundians

6th century:
The Franks

1st century BCE: The Roman Empire

10th century:
The Holy Roman Empire

Luckily, they chose to defend…and over the years, they learned how to do it incredibly well. If they hadn't, there would be no Switzerland today!

Here's how the game played itself out (in a nutshell)…

The Players

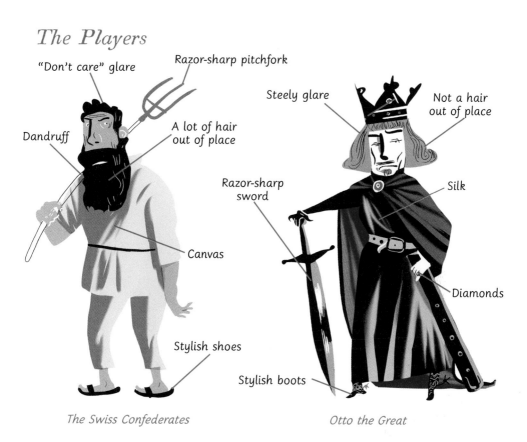

"Don't care" glare

Razor-sharp pitchfork

Steely glare

Not a hair out of place

Dandruff

A lot of hair out of place

Razor-sharp sword

Silk

Canvas

Diamonds

Stylish shoes

Stylish boots

The Swiss Confederates

Otto the Great

The Swiss Confederates

The people who lived in the region that is now known as modern Switzerland had several different names and ever-changing borders and allegiances over the centuries. However, when the Holy Roman Empire took control of the region at the end of the 10th century, communities, villages and towns came together to fight back against them. Cantons were born and, as their alliances grew, so did a confederation of Swiss communities... the Swiss Confederates.

The Horrific Holy Roman Empire
What a long name...let's just call it the HRE, ok?

During the Middle Ages, parts of what is now Switzerland belonged to one ruling family or another within the HRE. It all started with Otto the Great, king of Germany in the year 962. He got himself crowned emperor by the pope, and let rich, powerful families (Dynastic Families: see below) basically start pushing around everybody in the region. By 1032, all of current-day Switzerland belonged to the bossy H.R.E…and the locals were not too happy about it.

Dynastic Families
Like the big, bad, hideous Habsburgs

Yeah, you might have heard that name: Habsburgs. A bunch of them were appointed emperors of the Holy Roman Empire throughout the Middle Ages.

By the 13th century, the Habsburg family controlled all of Austria and many regions of modern-day Switzerland. Nice rulers they were not.

The Weapons

The Swiss halberd and instructions for using each part:

Fluke: the hooking bit. Good for dragging men off their horses in preparation for chop, chop.

Spike: the stabbing bit. Stab, stab and then chop, chop, if desired.

Langet: No langet, no chop, chop.

Long shaft: helps the user to perform chop, chop.

Axe blade: the chopping bit. Chop, chop.

The halberd was the invention of Swiss soldiers during the 14th century and their weapon of choice for years. It was wonderfully useful for dragging enemy horsemen to the ground, stabbing them through, and chopping them up quickly. They are still a ceremonial weapon of the Swiss Guards in the Vatican... although they're rarely used for stabbing or chopping any more.

Swiss dagger

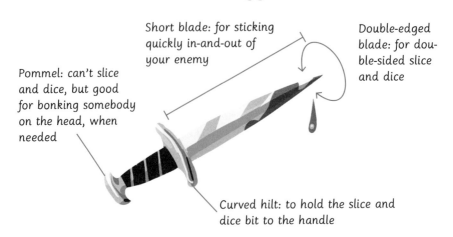

Short blade: for sticking quickly in-and-out of your enemy

Double-edged blade: for double-sided slice and dice

Pommel: can't slice and dice, but good for bonking somebody on the head, when needed

Curved hilt: to hold the slice and dice bit to the handle

The Swiss dagger was developed in Switzerland during the 14th and 15th centuries and used by Swiss mercenaries in close combat during the 16th century. So, if a Swiss mercenary wiggles his finger to draw you nearer, watch yourself.

The Swiss Pike Square

Get the point?

The Swiss Pike Square was a terrible thing to behold, and looked, according to some medieval sources, like a giant, angry hedgehog (in German, it's called the Igelstellung or Hedgehog defense). The men in the Pike Square were so well trained that a thousand of them could move at a dead run while maintaining perfect shoulder-to-shoulder formation. At the time, nothing and nobody could break the square, whether they were on foot, on horseback, or armed with swords. Add a few halberds to this already impressive square…and now imagine the opposing soldiers pooping their pants and running away.

Match the weapons with their purpose:

1. Halberd   A. Killing
2. Swiss Dagger   B. Killing
3. Swiss Pike Square   C. Killing

Answers: 1=ABC, 2=ABC, 3=ABC

The Beginning of Switzerland

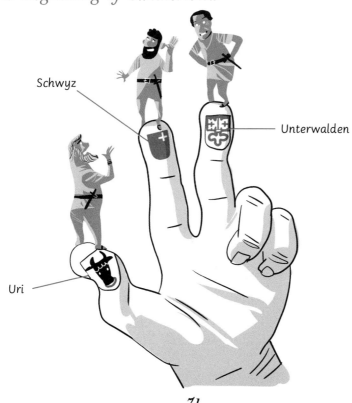

Schwyz

Unterwalden

Uri

71

By 1291, the people of what is now Switzerland said, "Enough of the HRE. We want our freedom." As the legend goes, on August 1st, 1291, representatives of three cantons (Uri, Schwyz, and Unterwalden) held a super-secret meeting in a meadow, promising to watch each other's backs and to defend each other against the HRE if it got too pushy. Well…the HRE got too pushy. So, defend each other they did…and,

the Swiss Confederacy was born.

But did it really happen like that? Nobody is quite sure. Nobody actually wrote anything about it all until years and years after it supposedly happened. The details were described in the White Book of Sarnen and the Chronicon Helveticum (yep, the same books that described William Tell and his shenanigans). That's the thing about myths and legends…sometimes they are only that, and nothing more. The reality was probably a bit different.

The Rütli Oath

After declaring their independence, the Confederates never looked back. The Holy Roman Emperor at the time, of course, thought the new Confederates were a bunch of poor hillbillies (which they basically were) and sent army after army to teach them a lesson. But he was the one who got schooled. Yes, the Confederates were poor. No, they didn't have much armor or many weapons. But they did have innovation, motivation, and loved their freedom more than life itself. So the Confederates managed to think up deadly ways to defend themselves using the materials they had.

The Battles and the Scorecard

The Swiss vs. the Habsburgs

1315: The Battle of Morgarten

Duke Leopold (one of the Habsburgs) sent 20,000 armored knights to crack down on the rebels. A mere 1,400 Confederate soldiers fought back, rolling huge boulders down a hill to squash the invaders, hacking any surviving knights to bits, and drowning whoever was left by shoving them down through a hole cut into an icy lake. In total, the Confederates killed 2000 of Duke Leo's soldiers, while losing only twelve of their own.

Scorecard

Holy Roman Empire 0

Confederates 1

1339: Battle of Laupen

6,500 Confederate foot soldiers tromped 12,000 Habsburg knights on horseback. Until then, soldiers on the ground had no chance against mounted knights. But the Confederates' tactics changed all that, and it didn't stop there. After the battle, they rounded-up all the surviving knights they could find and drowned them in the River Sense. Nobody is sure why. It probably just seemed to make sense.

Scorecard

Holy Roman Empire 0

Confederates 2

1386: Battle of Sempach

Duke Leopold III was the Habsburg Lord reigning over much of present-day Switzerland. He sent 4000 armored knights to squash those who wanted to be out from under his thumb. The Confederates fought back with 1300 of their own men. Most of them only had pieces of wood tied to their arms for armor, as well as a few halberds, but they were able to defeat the duke's army anyway, killing half of them, including Duke Leo III himself.

The legendary hero of the Battle of Sempach is Arnold von Winkelried. According to legend (which was probably just made up), the Confederates were unable to break the close ranks of the Habsburg pike men and thought they would lose the battle. Arnold von Winkelried reportedly cried out, "I will open a passage into the line. Protect, dear countrymen and confederates, my wife and children!" He then threw himself into the enemy's spears, taking as many into his own body as possible. Ouch. This broke up the front line of the Austrian troops and gave the Confederate warriors an opening through which to attack.

Scorecard

Holy Roman Empire 0

Confederates 3

1388: Battle of Näfels

The Habsburgs invaded with 15,000 men, but were defeated again by only 650 Confederates and another bunch of huge boulders rolling down a hill. In total, 1700 Habsburgs were squashed, stabbed, or sliced. The Confederates lost only a handful of men.

Scorecard

Holy Roman Empire 0

Confederates 4

Swiss vs. the Beastly Burgundians

After winning battle after battle against the horrific HRE, the Confederate warriors were becoming famous in Europe. But don't think for a moment that they laid down their weapons and started making cheese. They wanted to make sure all the other invaders stayed away as well.

The Dukes of Burgundy tried again and again to expand their power throughout parts of Europe. The last Duke of Burgundy, often called Charles the Bold or Charles the Liar, depending on who you were talking to (let's just call him Chuckie, shall we?), was aligned with the HRE. Chuckie decided to expand his territory into that of the Confederacy. That didn't sit well at all with the Confederates.

1476: Duke Chuckie at the Battle of Grandson

Chuckie besieged the castle of Grandson on the Lake of Neuchatel, promising the Confederate soldiers protecting the castle that their lives would be spared if they gave up. They did, and Chuckie had all 412 of them executed, hanging them from trees and drowning them in the lake. Liar. Well, too bad for Chuckie, because in the meantime, other Confederate troops who had no idea about the slaughter arrived to retake the castle. They defeated Chuckie's 20,000-man army relatively quickly, sending the most powerful army in Europe at the time into retreat. Afterwards, the Confederate soldiers found their murdered comrades freshly hung from trees or floating dead in the lake. This united them as never before and they swore revenge. Oh, and did they get it.

Scorecard

Burgundians 0

Confederates 1

1476: Battle of Murten

Chuckie re-organized and gathered an army of 23,000 to fight the Confederates again. The Confederates quickly mobilized an army of 25,000 and surprised Chuckie at Murten, killing thousands of his troops while only losing a few hundred of their own. Chuckie escaped that time, but his luck wouldn't last forever.

Chuckie the Horseman

1477: Duke Chuckie at the Battle of Nancy

The Confederates did not forget the Battle of Murten and were fiercer than ever at the Battle of Nancy. During the battle, an angry Confederate peasant with a halberd chopped Chuckie in the head, killing the last Duke of Burgundy. His body was found days later frozen into the nearby river. Chuckie's head had been cleft in two, lances were lodged in his stomach and groin, and his face had been so badly mutilated that his physician was only able to identify him by his long fingernails and the old battle scars on his body. That's one way to deal with liars. Before he got chopped, Chuckie is thought to have said, "I struggle against a spider who is everywhere at once," referring to the overwhelming power and fury of the angry Confederate troops.

Chuckie the Floater

Final Scorecard

Confederates: defended their independence

Burgundians / HRE / Habsburgs: got their butts kicked

If you haven't already memorized all these battles and dates and numbers of soldiers, you might like to get busy. There will be a test tomorrow morning.

BE READY

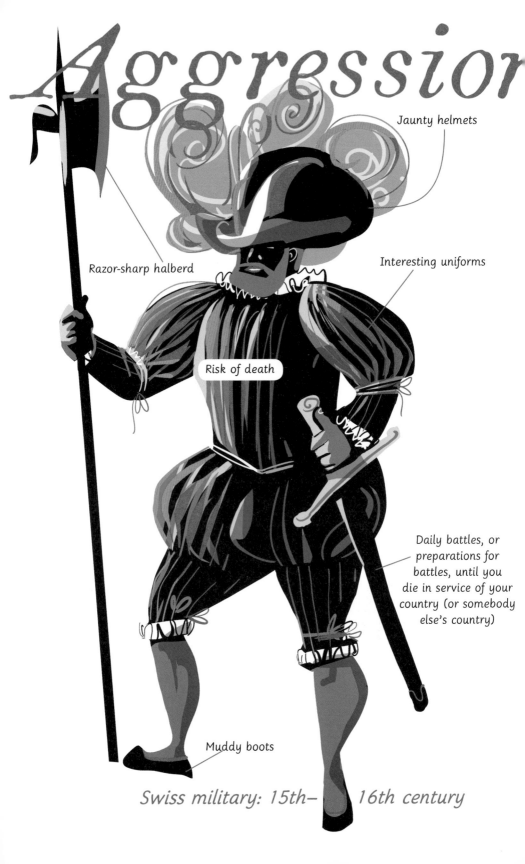

Aggression

Jaunty helmets

Razor-sharp halberd

Interesting uniforms

Risk of death

Daily battles, or preparations for battles, until you die in service of your country (or somebody else's country)

Muddy boots

Swiss military: 15th– 16th century

to Armed Neutrality

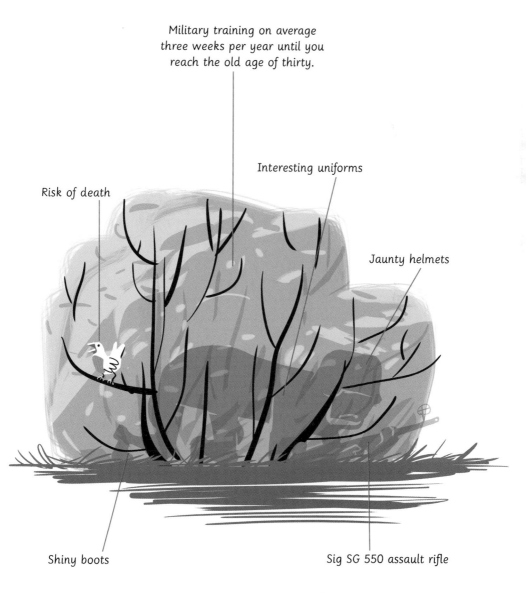

Military training on average three weeks per year until you reach the old age of thirty.

Interesting uniforms

Risk of death

Jaunty helmets

Shiny boots

Sig SG 550 assault rifle

Swiss military: modern

Now don't go getting the idea that the Swiss were so completely absorbed in defending themselves from the horrid Habsburgs, the beastly Burgundians, and others that they didn't have an aggressive plan or two of their own. Nope. C'mon, it was the Late Middle Ages...the time of European conquests! Everybody was grabbing land from everybody else. The Holy Roman Empire was quite busy conquering left and right. The Ottoman Empire was spreading across southeastern Europe after conquering what remained of the Byzantine Empire. England was facing off against the French, the Scots, and then the French again. Europe was busy playing the medieval power game and the Swiss were no exception. Sorry to break it to you.

At the time they broke free from Habsburg rule, the Swiss Confederacy was made up of eight cantons—Bern, Lucerne, Zurich, Zug, Glarus, Schwyz, Uri, and the two half-cantons of Obwalden and Nidwalden. There were lots of empty spaces in between what already belonged to the Swiss Confederacy.

The Swiss Confederacy's plan for expansion

So, wherever the Swiss Confederacy could make agreements and friendly alliances, they did. For example, the so-called "Three Leagues" to the southeast (which is now Canton Graubünden) were also immersed in battles against the greedy Habsburgs when they decided to become allies with the Swiss Confederacy. This was an important friendship, as it gave the Swiss Confederacy access to, and control of, the mountain passes to the east of the Gotthard Pass.

Likewise, Lucerne, Uri, Nidwalden, and Obwalden allied themselves with Valais, which gave the Confederacy control over the area west of the Gotthard Pass.

All this basically meant that the Swiss Confederacy controlled nearly all routes of travel north and south of the Alps

But some of the other regions didn't want to come along so easily. In 1402, Uri attacked and conquered the Levantine Valley in Ticino, taking it as a territory...like it or not. In 1415, the Confederates attacked Aargau to fill in the space between Bern, Lucerne and Zurich, clicking it into place like the piece that was always missing from the middle of a jigsaw puzzle.

Making friends in 1415

Why were the Swiss Confederates doing this? After centuries of having to defend themselves against foreign powers on all sides, fighting off Romans, Franks, Habsburgs, Burgundians, Savoyards, etc., etc., etc...well...the Swiss had become really, really good at battle. They had a nearly unbroken record of military success for the past two hundred years. They were good...and they knew it.

There was a lot to be proud of. Between 1400 and 1500, the Confederacy had grown from a tiny, loosely organized collection of cantons to an impressive political power on the European stage. By 1500, the Swiss Confederacy was negotiating treaties with the major powers of Europe, including Habsburg Emperors, Kings of France, and more. They'd come a long, long way from the poor peasants they'd used to be.

The Swiss Confederacy grows...

After so much success, it naturally all went a bit to their heads. The Swiss Confederacy became ever more aggressive…and then they aimed a little too high.

The Swiss Confederacy sets its sights on Milan

In the centuries since it was founded in 400 BCE, Milan had been in the hands of Celts, Romans, Goths, Lombards, Spaniards, and Austrians. By the 14th century, the Duchy of Milan was THE great financial and political power in northern Italy.

Back in 1495, the Swiss Confederates accepted a deal with Louis of Orleans from France. He'd promised them control of Bellinzona, Lugano, Locarno, and Arona. The Swiss Confederates knew that control of these regions would get them that much closer to Milan. Good deal, no? In return, they had to supply Louis of Orleans with Swiss mercenary soldiers to fight alongside his own troops, anywhere he wanted. Handshake. Done.

Four years later and the truth came out. Louis of Orleans—now Louis XII, King of France—took most of the promised regions for himself...and then grabbed Milan too.

The Swiss Confederates were understandably ticked-off at King Louis XII and decided to get their revenge. They befriended Pope Julius II, Louis' archenemy, just to make Louis nuts. The Pope had already founded the Swiss Guard, an elite troop made up of a constant corps of Swiss mercenaries to protect Vatican City and the Pope himself. Now he enlisted the Swiss mercenaries to kick King Louis XII's butt out of Milan, which they were only too happy to do.

Revenge is sweet

One year later, at the end of 1512, the Swiss mercenaries installed Maxmilian Sforza as the new duke of Milan. Six months later, King Louis XII besieged the city of Novara to the west of Milan. The Swiss mercenaries were only too happy to show up and kick his butt again. In the process, they were able to add more parts of southern Ticino to the growing list of Swiss territories.

Two years later, in 1515, the Swiss Confederacy got just a little too big for its britches

France had a new ruler—King François I—who intended to have Milan for himself. He also had artillery that was devastatingly powerful…much more deadly than anything the Swiss soldiers had at that time. But no matter.

The leaders of the Swiss Confederates met with King François I and negotiated a deal. France would get Milan. No battle would be fought. Everybody could live to fight another day. But that's not what happened.

The Swiss Confederates who were present during the negotiations had no plans to fight the French. But then additional troops arrived on the scene. They'd just marched for days over the Alps to take part in this battle and had no intention of leaving empty-handed. They got the rest of the troops worked up and, despite the agreement made with the French, they decided to go for it.

Sorry. We lied.

The Swiss Confederates marched on the French troops in the town of Marignano. The French, thinking the negotiations were done and dusted, were not expecting the attack. Nevertheless, they assembled quickly and fought back. The two armies fought into the night until they couldn't see each other anymore. Both armies reorganized and rested until dawn, and then the fighting started again. By noon it was all over. After more than sixteen hours of bloody battle, the Swiss Confederates had already lost about half of their 22,000 soldiers and were forced to retreat. The Battle of Marignano was lost to the French.

From the Swiss Confederate point of view, the lesson was learned. Their 200-year domination on the battlefields of Europe was over. They knew that they simply could not compete with the big boys anymore.

In 1516, the Swiss Confederacy signed a "perpetual peace" treaty with France. As part of the deal, France got unlimited access to Swiss mercenary soldiers (who anyway didn't have too much to do anymore).

The Swiss Confederacy promised never to battle against France again. They also got to keep Ticino.

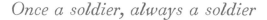

Once a soldier, always a soldier

This was the one of the many steps towards Switzerland becoming the neutral country we know today. Yes, Swiss troops continued to fight on behalf of the French for the next couple hundred years, but they did not try to expand their own territory again.

Quite the opposite. The Swiss government eventually decided that "the best offense is a good defense." So, instead of trying to expand their territory and power, they invested tons of energy and cash into ensuring that the land and power they already had stayed that way. The Swiss will not fight in any war unless they are directly attacked...and attacking them would be costly, as the army is constantly armed and ready to mobilize quickly to respond to any threat. Even today. But, OK, back to the Swiss Confederacy.

The Swiss Confederate soldiers—trained for battle and suddenly finding themselves with lots of time on their hands—found something else to do. They started enlisting—more than ever before—as mercenaries in the armies of other European nations. As it turned out, there were still a lot of battles to fight.

The spoils of war

Not sure what mercenaries are? Read on, my friend.

Mercy, Please,

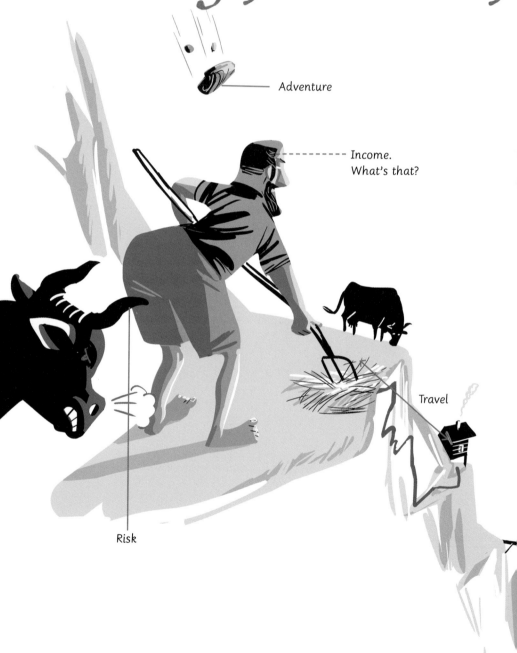

Adventure

Income.
What's that?

Travel

Risk

Swiss at home

Mercenaries

Travel

PARIS

TOKIO

ROMA

Adventure

Risk

Income.
Bingo!

Swiss mercenary

A mercenary is simply a soldier who is paid to fight for the army of another country. Often called "soldiers of fortune," they are not usually interested in the reason the war is being fought. Instead, their main interest is in getting paid to fight it.

Reasons for mercenaries to fight for foreign nations

God

Country

~~Honor~~

~~Love~~

~~Revenge~~

Cash

Why would a foreign army want to hire soldiers from other nations to fight their wars? Simple, really...

1. Their own troops have already been decimated

OK, now you go!

2. They want to intimidate the enemy

3. To keep from losing their own troops

It's not a new concept. The armies of Europe had been using mercenaries for hundreds of years. It might surprise you to know that Switzerland was one of the biggest and most impressive suppliers of mercenaries for about five hundred years. It's estimated that the Swiss provided well over one million mercenaries to fight for foreign armies between the 14th and 19th centuries.

Mercenaries here! Get your mercenaries! They're young, they're strong, they're dying to fight your war. Get 'em while they last!

So why the Swiss? Why were they the best ones to have fighting in your army? Well, as we know, the Swiss had been forced to defend themselves and their land pretty much since the beginning of time. By the Late Middle Ages (in the 1300s), the Swiss had become top notch at warfare. Their greatest trick of the trade was something they invented and perfected out of necessity...
the Swiss Pike Square.

The square of death

The Swiss were not rich at this point in history. They didn't have suits of armor, chain mail, or big, expensive weapons. But they were innovative and they were brave...and the Pike Square they invented was a death machine.

This mass of soldiers would grab their weapons, form a quick square, and launch themselves at their enemy. They could walk, run, and change direction as a single unit, stabbing and chopping anything and anybody that got in their way. Their opponents, if they weren't speared through the middle immediately, were either chopped up by halberds, trampled to death, or stabbed with daggers as the Swiss Pike Square tromped its way through. No hostages were taken. It's been said that the only things coming out the back end of a Swiss Pike Square were corpses. In the 1300s, nobody had seen anything quite like it.

The most common screech of horror heard on battlefields during the High Middle Ages

THE SWISS ARE COMING!

If that weren't already enough, many mercenaries were issued a double-edged, short-handled Swiss dagger for sinking into their enemies' guts.

Small talk during battle

It's standard issue, but I think it's great! The subtle curve of the hilt makes all the difference.

After proving themselves on the battlefields and kicking the collective Habsburg butt, Burgundian butt, and every other type of butt, Swiss mercenary troops were a hot item. France, Austria, Savoy, Hungary and even the Pope clamored to get them for their own armies.

Back in 1506, Pope Julius II hired Swiss mercenaries to protect both him and the Vatican from evil-doers. Popes in those days were not the peace-loving figureheads of the Catholic Church we expect today. They owned vast territories, commanded armies, and didn't worry much about those armies committing massive amounts of violence, as long as the Pope got whatever it was that he wanted. Well, Pope Julius II wanted, and got, his Swiss mercenaries. No less than 150 of them marched across the Alps from Switzerland, arriving for duty in Rome on January 22nd, 1506. The Swiss Guard got their first on-the-job challenge soon afterwards, during the Sack of Rome in 1527.

34,000 angry Habsburg soldiers trashed Rome and looted everything they could get their hands on. They also wanted to go get the Pope himself, but the Swiss Guards would not let that happen. Most of the Swiss Guards were slaughtered while protecting the Pope, but the few who survived managed to sneak the Pope to safety through a secret stone passageway. From then on it was clear. Future Popes would definitely keep their Swiss Guard. An ever-changing Swiss Guard has protected the Pope and the Vatican ever since.

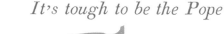

It's tough to be the Pope

Around this time the Swiss suffered their horribly embarrassing defeat at Marignano, Italy, and started to rethink their ideas about conquering territories and expanding (see last chapter). Lots of soldiers were suddenly out of work. What do you do when you're a trained soldier with no wars to fight anymore? Go fight wars for other countries and get paid handsomely to do it!

The Swiss fighting for cash all over Europe

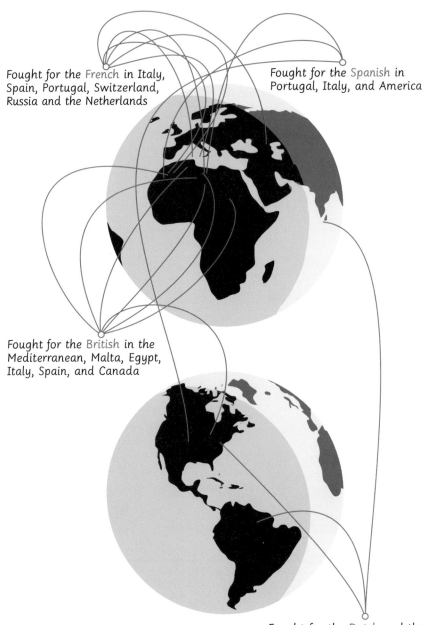

Fought for the French in Italy, Spain, Portugal, Switzerland, Russia and the Netherlands

Fought for the Spanish in Portugal, Italy, and America

Fought for the British in the Mediterranean, Malta, Egypt, Italy, Spain, and Canada

Fought for the Dutch and the Dutch East India Company in the Cape Colony and the East Indies, Surinam and Canada. Guards at the Dutch Royal Palace from 1815–1829

In 1848, Switzerland adopted its first official constitution, which prohibited any new contracts for Swiss mercenaries in foreign countries. In 1859, if the existing mercenaries hadn't already died in one battle or another, it was time to go home or search for new adventures elsewhere. All mercenary service became illegal. Except, of course, for one exception.

It's good to be the Pope

We can't take the Swiss Guard away from him. He's best buddies with God!

So why did young, strong Swiss men put their lives on the line to become mercenary soldiers? For those hiring themselves out to foreign nations, the answer was clear—money. Back in those days, Switzerland was one of the poorest countries in Europe. So these guys sold their strengths—the best of which was their ability to fight. Swiss mercenaries were paid more than any other type of mercenary purely because they were so very lethal... and lethal is what you want when you're commanding armies.

Also, mercenaries were adventurers and were ready to conquer a wider world than the little villages where they grew up.

Occupational hazard #1

Some were tricked into signing mercenary contracts and suddenly found themselves holding a pike and running into battle.

Occupational hazard #2

But most were professional soldiers who were offering their services for hire according to a contract. They earned a living from a respectable job in the largest industry at the time in Europe.

Swiss mercenaries hired themselves out either as individuals or entire units, complete with weapons. Kings and generals competed to hire them. Quite often, two or more bullying countries would get into bidding wars to see who could get the Swiss mercenaries on their side. This meant that, sometimes, Swiss mercenaries would fight against other Swiss mercenaries.

Occupational hazard #3

It's not quite the same for the Pope's Swiss Guards at the Vatican these days. Yes, they are paid well, but all of the guards must belong to the Catholic religion, whether they are practicing Catholics or not. Some believe there is no higher honor for a Catholic than to protect the Pope and the Vatican. Others have just always dreamt of being in the Swiss Guard.

In order to be a Swiss guardsman, they must also be:

Between the ages of
19 and 30 years old

Unmarried and celibate

At least 1.74 meters tall

The latest development for the Swiss Guards is quite the fashion statement. The cast-iron helmets that the guards traditionally wear are about to become a thing of the past. The newest helmets will be 3D-printed in plastic, will be less than half the weight of the old helmets, and will no longer singe the guards' heads when they're standing outside in the Roman summer sun.

Occupational hazard #4

Food Fights

The Disgusting Cow Tongue War of 1859

The Stinky Fondue War of 1928

The Glorious Ice Cream War of 2019

The Potato Ditch War of...since longer than anybody can remember

Real foodie battles

While Confederate soldiers were busy kicking butt on the battle-grounds of Europe, life back in the medieval cities, towns, and villages of Switzerland was changing quickly. Peasants in the countryside started organizing their own local governments, while the rich and powerful people in the cities kept doing what the rich and powerful often do…they took advantage of the peasants by taxing their socks off. That way, the rich kept themselves rich, while the poor got poorer and poorer (and poorer).

Poor guy is getting his socks taxed off…

Beware, the 1513 War of the Onions in Lucerne!

Take Lucerne, for example. When the poor got poorer—and ticked off—enough…

Step one: People in cities get rich and then build big houses with nice vegetable gardens

Step two: Poor peasants get poorer and then get ticked off

Step three: Thousands of angry peasants storm Lucerne

Step four: Peasants stomp on gardens. Throw vegetables about.

There's no proof of what kinds of vegetables were actually destroyed, or whether onions were the rioters' key weapons. So why it wasn't called The Carrot Capers or The French Bean Fiasco, the world will never know. Maybe because it was old onions smell really gross, uprooted and rotting in the sun. Or maybe a few rioters had stinky onion breath. Anyway, the riots ended when dozens of the rioters were arrested and their leader got his own onion chopped off at the neck. But it wasn't over yet. Other peasants in Switzerland had been watching.

At least it took care of his onion breath...

The 1515 Gingerbread War of Zurich

Two years later, similar revolts broke out in Zurich. This time, the frustrated peasants plundered shops and market stalls near Zurich's Market Square in an area known for selling sweets and gingerbread, earning the chaos the title of "The Gingerbread War." Apparently, the peasants were getting smarter...and probably a little chubbier...stuffing their faces with gingerbread this time, instead of onions. It probably didn't smell very sweet to the shop owners, though.

I knew I should have switched to selling face cream...

The Affair of the Sausages in 1522

Huldrych Zwingli was pastor of the Grossmünster in Zurich, where he was known as a talented, but odd, sort of guy. He spoke out against the church's practice of promising to keep people out of hell if they gave a ton of money to the church—which really pissed off all the corrupt church leaders.

Then things got worse. Zwingli and some of his friends took a stand against the Catholic Church "law" about which foods could be eaten during Lent, the time before Easter. Instead of eating fish, as dictated by the church, they sat down together in secret one evening to eat...can you guess?

Nobody saw them do it, but they made sure to spread the word afterwards that they had eaten...two smoked sausages. Gasp!

The man who hosted the event, Christoph Froschauer, was immediately arrested. Zwingli wasn't, as apparently he hadn't eaten any of the sausages himself. Don't ask how they checked that out! But Zwingli did deliver a fiery sermon two weeks later called "Regarding the choice and freedom of foods," shouting out that the Bible does not state what you should—and should not—eat.

16th century Airport Sausage Control

The people of Zurich freaked out. Fights erupted in taverns and in the streets. All of that for sausages.

The Catholic Bishop of Constance sent a bunch of his men to see what all the fuss was about. Zwingli met the delegation and announced that Zurich would no longer follow the fasting rules of the Catholic Church. It worked. Within a year, forced fasting was abolished in Zurich and sausages could be eaten freely again... all because of two smoked sausages and an odd man with an attitude.

First War of Kappel in 1529

No, the outcome of the sausage story didn't mean that the issues between the Catholics and non-Catholics were over. Nooo, not by a long shot. A new form of Christian religion called "Protestanism" was rising throughout Europe. Protestants were protesting against the things that they didn't like about the Catholic Church. In Zurich, Zwingli led the Protestants...at least for a while.

Over time, tensions got so bad between the Catholics and the Protestants in Switzerland that they eventually went to war with each other. But the first of the wars was actually no war at all.

Zwingli teamed up with other Protestant cantons in Switzerland. Catholic cantons teamed-up with the Holy Roman Emperor, Ferdinand of Austria. They threatened each other, shouting back and forth a bit without really doing much fighting... until a Catholic priest was executed within Protestant territory in 1528. The Catholics responded by burning a Protestant pastor at the stake in 1529. Eventually, Protestant Zurich declared war against the Catholic cantons in 1529. Troops from both sides met at Kappel, near the border of Zug, ready to fight, and then...waited.

Mediators from both sides were sent to discuss the situation. Apparently, they took their sweet time. While the mediation went on and on, the soldiers on both sides got bored. They chatted together, drank together, all the while waiting to hear their fate—

fight each other, or not. Then they got hungry, too. The Protestant army had bread. The Catholic army had milk. So, while the mediators blathered on, the armies cooked and ate a warm meal of milk soup together.

Yup, that's the whole story. No blood, guts, or flying vegetables. Just warm milk soup.

But if you think those religious men were going to stop with warm soup, you're wrong. Less than two years later, there was re-do: The Second War of Kappel. Zwingli and twenty-four other pastors were killed and then the victorious Catholics burned Zwingli's corpse for good measure.

Mère Royaume's famous vegetable soup

During the darkest part of the night between December 11th and 12th in the year 1602, the Duke of Savoy from France decided to launch a surprise attack against Geneva. The duke's father was so stubborn that he'd earned the name Ironhead, and the son also knew exactly what he wanted.

Here is what he wanted:

So, after his tantrum was over, the duke ordered his troops to attack in the middle of the night, hoping shock and surprise would win the day.

*But he had a few shocks and surprises waiting for him,
notably in the form of a woman named Mère Royaume.*

Catherine Cheynel (also known as Mère Royaume since she was
married to Mr. Royaume) was a sixty-year-old mother of fourteen
children. As the legend goes, she was cooking a large cauldron of
vegetable soup that night when she saw the duke's men scaling
the walls of the city. She grabbed her cauldron of steaming hot
soup, ran to the city walls, and dumped it onto the attackers.
She managed to scald a lot of them, sending them tumbling back
down the wall in pain. She even killed one when she dropped
the heavy cauldron on his head.

When Mère Royaume's soup hit the duke's soldiers, their screams of pain woke everybody up.

Men, women, and children fought back, forcing the duke's army to retreat and killing fifty-four of them in the process.

Thirteen of the duke's soldiers were taken prisoner that night and hanged in the morning…without even so much as a bowl of soup first.

It was worth it. This soup is awesome.

For the past 400 years, Geneva has commemorated L'Escalade (that means "the scaling" in French) with a two-day celebration. Chocolate cauldrons (called "marmites") are wrapped in ribbons of red and gold, the colors of Geneva, and stuffed with sweets and marzipan vegetables to celebrate Mère Royaume's very famous vegetable soup.

Keep Calm and

Solutions for bad things happening because of magic

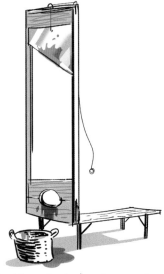

Problem: Bad year for crops?
Solution: It must be the stuttering fellow in the hovel next door.
Off with his head! Chop, chop!

Problem: Hailstorm causes famine?
Solution: It must be the odd woman with the creepy herb garden.
Burn her at the stake! That should solve things.

Carry a Wand

Problem: Cow stopped giving milk?
Solution: It must be that attractive woman next door.
Your husband keeps ogling her and drooling.
Report her. Then watch her get hanged to death.

Problem: You got a smelly rash on your foot?
Solution: It must be those weird immigrants settling in the village.
Drive them out! Or chop their heads off. Whatever.

What does all this have to do with Switzerland, you might ask? Well, as it turns out, the region of the world that is today known as tidy, rational, neutral Switzerland was nothing of the sort way back when. Remember, during the Middle Ages and the Reformation, what we call Switzerland was a land of mostly poor, uneducated peasants who were struggling for survival. Many people believed in black magic and were ready to do *anything* to protect themselves and their families.

Of course, this is all true for Europe, in general. But for some reason, in the heyday of witch hunts from 1550 to 1700, there were more accusations of witchcraft and executions of witches in Switzerland than anywhere else in Europe.

By the 16th century...

Swiss executions

All others

Of the 80,000 people accused of witchcraft across Europe, a whopping 10,000 of them were in what is present-day Switzerland. Two-thirds of those accused were executed. That's 6000 people burned at the stake.

That's a lot of dead Swiss witches and warlocks.

Most of those accused of witchcraft were women. About 75% Of course! Since when have women ever had a fair shake? As you might have guessed, little or no proof of actual witchcraft was required. Bad deal for the accused.

So, why were regular people accused of something so ridiculous? And why mostly women? It all comes down to power. Who had it? Who didn't? Who wanted it? Who thought others had too much?

But these are only examples. Who were some of these actual unlucky souls?

Soulmother of Küssnacht (executed 1577)

Not much is known about the Soulmother of Küssnacht—not even her real name. Any records that show her name have long disappeared for whatever reason. All that's known is that the Soulmother of Küssnacht was an elderly lady with a cool nickname and a strange gift.

From about 1560, the Soulmother got a reputation for being able to speak with the dead. When someone died, their friends and relatives would rush to visit the Soulmother, who had visions and could speak to the dead person's spirit. She would find answers to the questions of the living and advise them on how the dead person wanted to be buried.

When customers arrived at her door, the Soulmother would first speak with them and gather information about the dead person. Then she would send the customers to stay in a nearby guesthouse run by her friend, Verena Lifibach, often filling it to the last bed. If only Airbnb was up and running back then in Küssnacht...they would have made a fortune.

Talk to your dead dog	CHF 20
Throw a stick for your dead dog	CHF 10
Talk to a dead person	CHF 30
Throw a stick for a dead person	CHF 25

The Soulmother's services became so popular that the local priests took notice. After all, she was competing for their customers... the grieving family members who needed to be reminded of God's eternal awesomeness, *not* the Soulmother's talents. The priests sent a letter of complaint to the Bishop. The Soulmother went to trial for her "non-Christian fantasies." After a bit of torture (which always helps to loosen the tongue), she confessed to witchcraft, was found guilty, and was burned alive at the stake.

Michée Chauderon (1602-1652)

Michée was a flawed fifty-year old washerwoman in Geneva.

It was just a matter of time for poor old Michée. One day Michée's employers accused her of stealing some linens and Michée chose to argue. They said she'd summoned a demon into the body of their daughter.

Here were all the things wrong with Michée:

Poor

Illiterate

An immigrant

5 — Spoke her mind

Tended to summon demons into children

4

Michée
Chauderon
1602

And then they found proof that she was certainly a witch.

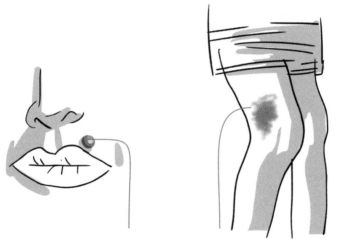

She had a mole on her upper lip and a strange growth on her thigh!*
*Everyone knows that means you're a witch.

Michée was tortured by strappado.
That's sounds like fun,

BUT IT'S NOT.

Here is how it works:
Her hands were tied behind her back.
She was lifted off the ground by a rope attached to her wrists.
Because it hurt so much, she said anything they wanted. She said (or perhaps screamed) that she had met with Satan in her garden.
Now they knew she was a witch. So, she was hanged to death.
Then she was burned, just be sure.

Luckily for the other poor, illiterate, odd folks in Geneva, she was the last person executed for witchcraft there. Well, up till now...

Catherine Répond – "The Catillon" (1663-1731)

The bailiff for the town of Villargiroud was a bad hunter. In 1730, he injured a fox on the paw, but didn't quite kill it. As it scampered off, he was sure he heard it yell, "Ow! My foot!" That was strange, because most foxes can't talk.

As he was riding home, he saw Catherine Répond.

Why he was sure she was a witch...

Hiding in forest from bad weather

Hunchbacked

Begging for food

Hurt foot

You get the point. Obviously, she was a witch who could shapeshift into a fox!

The bailiff had her arrested and tortured until she confessed that she had flown on a broomstick to the witches' Sabbath. She was taken to Fribourg, found guilty of witchcraft, and strangled to death. The sanity of the bailiff, who claimed to have heard a fox speaking, was never questioned.

Also, apparently nobody minded that he was a very bad shot.

Anna Göldi (1734–1782)

This woman is probably the most famous "witch" in Switzerland. Born into a poor family, Anna worked as a maid.

She had two children and she wasn't married and so she got what she "deserved"

She was put in a pillory in the middle of the village so everyone could laugh at her.

Her children were taken away from her.

2 Kids NOT married!

In 1780 Anna found a job as a maid with the Tschudi family. Mr. Tschudi was a rich politician with tons of influence who abused Anna for fun.

Here's about how that went...

Two weeks later...

127

During torture, Anna admitted to entering into a pact with the devil, who had appeared to her as a dog. When her torture was finished, she withdrew her confession, but it was too late. Even though it was the beginning of the Age of Enlightenment and superstition was being ridiculed, people were hungry for one more witch decapitation. And they got it. Anna was the last person to be executed for witchcraft in Switzerland.

It's the 1780s, guys.
Do torture and decapitation still make sense?

Napoleon

Switzerland before Napoleon

Cantons battle against cantons

Switzerland with Napoleon

Cantons battle against French

Switzerland after Napoleon

Cantons battle against cantons

Bozo aristocrats

No national flag

Bozo dictator

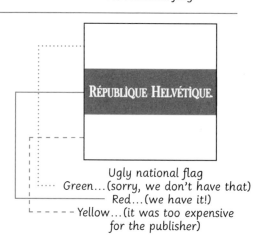

Ugly national flag
Green...(sorry, we don't have that)
Red...(we have it!)
Yellow...(it was too expensive
for the publisher)

Bozo politicians

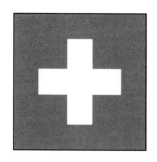

Swiss flag

French soldiers invaded the Swiss Confederacy in 1798. It wasn't very hard. They just marched across the eastern border without any major hassle. Many of those living in Geneva, Lausanne, and Basel just let the soldiers pass. Some actually cheered. No blood, no guts, no battle cries.

The French guy responsible for this invasion was Napoleon Bonaparte, a military leader who was perhaps history's most famous conqueror. Napoleon was hungry for success—and hopeful he could take a big piece of Swiss Pie for France.

The parts of Bonaparte

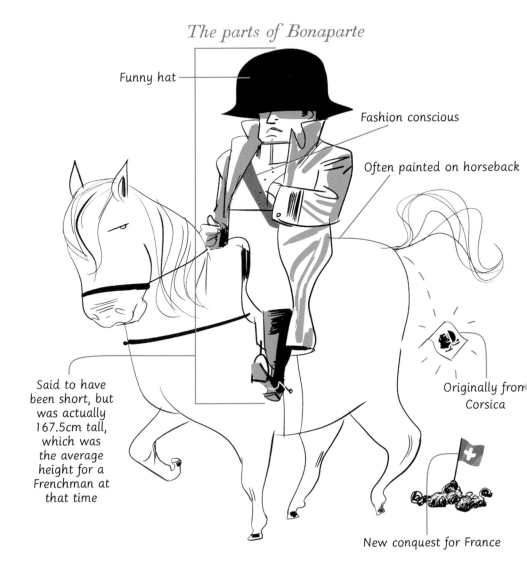

Funny hat

Fashion conscious

Often painted on horseback

Said to have been short, but was actually 167.5cm tall, which was the average height for a Frenchman at that time

Originally from Corsica

New conquest for France

Nine years earlier, in 1789, France had gone through a revolution. The people wanted a country where every man was free and equal. So they chased away the powerful, wealthy men controlling the country, overthrew the monarchy, and sent King Louis XVI and Queen Marie Antoinette to have their heads chopped off by the guillotine. Rumor has it that King Louis shifted a little in the guillotine and the blade missed his neck. It went through the back of his skull and chopped through his jaw. Ouch.

France was rebuilt as a republic of the people where everyone was free and equal.

Fighting for freedom and equality in 1789

Us, too?

But of course not, silly woman!

Napoleon, at the time, was generally admired in a few of the Swiss cantons where people were also fed up with being bossed around by their own rich, stuffy oligarchs. In fact, as Napoleon rode through Switzerland on his way to a Peace Congress in Germany in November 1797, people in Geneva, Lausanne, and Basel actually lined the streets to give him a Hero's Welcome.

Little did anybody know at the time, but Napoleon already had plans in his pocket for the invasion and takeover of Switzerland. He'd cooked up his plans with two Swiss guys who were unhappy with how things were going in the Swiss Confederacy, Frédéric-César de La Harpe and Peter Ochs.

In December 1797, Napoleon met La Harpe (from Vaud) and Peter Ochs (from Basel) for dinner. They made plans for a new Swiss republic, complete with a new constitution...and then they made it happen.

On December 28th, 1797, the French warned the government in Bern that they were placing Vaud under its protection and that troops were on the way. The government in Bern, without the support of its neighboring cantons, did nothing to prevent it. When the time came for the French troops to march into Bern, it was like taking candy from a baby.

The French invasion of Bern

Unfortunately, word of Bern's quiet acceptance of the situation didn't reach the villagers in the Bernese countryside...who were ready to defend their land with their lives. The following day in Grauholz about 6400 farmers, their wives, and their children stood up to 18,000 invading French soldiers. Those poor villagers never stood a chance and were massacred in about two and a half hours.

2000 Swiss were massacred at the Battle of Grauholz

Napoleon rebranded the Swiss Confederacy as the Helvetic Republic. Then he set about re-organizing everything. He set up a new, shiny centralized government, including a parliament and a supreme court. He also put together the country's first constitution with a little help from his friends, La Harpe and Ochs. For the first time, the country was a nation of citizens who were well-organized, had (some) equality, could choose their own government officials, and could even vote on changes to their own constitution.

Napoleon also ensured:

Freedom of the press

Uniform weights and measures in metric

A reliable postal service

Well…as reliable as a postal service can be.

And that the first national currency was introduced

It worked. For a while. But despite all the positive things that Napoleon brought the people of the new Helvetic Republic, there were negatives. And they got more and more negative as time went on. During the next five years, the Helvetic Republic never actually managed to become a stable nation.

Eventually things got totally out of hand. The economy collapsed. To make things even worse, the Helvetic Republic found itself forced to fight for France whenever France wanted. That essentially ended Swiss neutrality and made a lot of people very, very angry. Battles on Swiss soil ravaged the land and ruined crops. Farmers couldn't farm their land if people kept running all over it shooting each other. During the winter of 1799–1800, many people were starving. Something had to change.

Soon after, Napoleon decided to withdraw French troops and leave the Helvetic Republic to its fate.

Let's get out of here before they start complaining again!

The moment Napoleon left the Helvetic Republic, things got even worse. Rebels who wanted to go back to the old ways revolted against the newly-formed armies of the Helvetic Republic. Since Napoleon had taken most of the artillery with him when he left, some of the rebels were armed only with sticks and clubs.

The War of Sticks of 1802*

*Yes, this is really what it was called.

Napoleon finally realized that with its different languages, different religions, and different cultures, Switzerland was designed by nature to be a federation of cantons...and nothing else.

In October of 1802, Napoleon decided to compromise with the rebels. He imposed the Act of Mediation, which would reduce the power of the central government and restore some power to the cantons.

The Helvetic Republic was dissolved, and the Act of Mediation was imposed during February of 1803. It remained in force until 1813, at which time Napoleon was off invading Russia and getting his butt solidly kicked in the process.

As part of the Act of Mediation, Napoleon also:
- pulled the cantons into one nation
- created a Swiss citizenship
- added six new cantons
- allowed people of different religions to marry
- improved the educational system
- improved public services
- and ensured:
    - equality of all citizens before the law
    - equality of the Swiss national languages
    - freedom of thought, speech, and religion

In 1814, the cantonal constitutions were re-written, bearing in mind all the improvements that had been introduced by Napoleon.

Thirty-four years later, in 1848, the Swiss Confederation wrote and adopted its own federal constitution, some of which was based on the agreements made in Napoleon's Act of Mediation. Finally, what had been the Helvetic Republic became Switzerland. And so it remains—more or less—to this day.

Direct

Democracy

→ Democracy

Swiss democracy

Once Napoleon left what we call Switzerland in 1802, things were peaceful for a short while. But before long, fights broke out again between the cantons. It was kind of like when a teacher leaves kids alone in a classroom for a while...

Total mayhem

But in this case the teacher (Mr. Napoleon) never came back into the classroom. The country was very much on its own, with no ruler, a messy government, and lots and lots of opinions about what to do next.

There were two main opinions about how to organize the country's new government—and Switzerland found itself bitterly divided. Many cantons (especially the rich people within them) wanted to return to the old, pre-Napoleon ways. That was when the rich got to boss around the poor, and each canton (especially the rich people within them) got to make up its own rules and laws (as long as they benefitted the rich).

Other cantons, especially the newest ones to join the Swiss Confederation, had fresh ideas.

They wanted to give democracy a chance and give every <u>man</u> more power and freedoms

After years of arguments and wars between the cantons, Switzerland had to choose.

There was a lot of fighting and arguing, but in 1848 Switzerland had its own constitution

This meant that the government was not an all-powerful giant controlling the entire land. Instead, power is shared between the central government in Bern, all the cantons that make up Switzerland, and the many municipalities within each canton.

Whenever there are choices to be made, the people of Switzerland get to vote for—or against—those choices. They can request changes to existing laws made by the government. They even have the right to suggest completely new laws, which then get voted on. This gives "little people" power over laws that affect them. That's a good thing.

In 1848, modern Switzerland was born. Citizens (as long as they were men) got tons of rights and freedoms, no matter how rich or poor they happened to be. It didn't matter if they lived in the biggest cities or the smallest villages.

So, Switzerland became a democracy. But what exactly is "direct democracy?"

Raise your hand if you'd like me to tell you.

Cool. Hand up or hand down, you've just participated in a vote using direct democracy. Good job. Now you understand it.

Congratulations.

Put your hands down.

Chapter over.

HA! FOOLED YOU!

Direct democracy is just a bit more complicated than that. Fooled you again! It's a LOT more complicated than that! Gotcha.

First, let's look at the word "direct."
That's kind of simple, isn't it?
"Direct" means...

Now let's look at the word "democracy." You remember what that is, right? We just talked about it. Keep up. Geez.

People who live in a democracy get to vote for—or against—the things that are important to them. That could mean, for example:

- Students in a sports class voting on what game to play for the next hour.

- A family voting about which pastries to buy for their artery-clogging breakfast on Sunday mornings.

- People of a nation voting on stuff that's important to them.

Democracy in five easy steps:

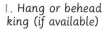

1. Hang or behead king (if available)

2. Get everyone together (and I mean everyone— even women)

3. Ask everyone: Should everyone have to eat cream every Sunday?

4. Count hands

5. Force everyone to eat ice cream and talk about how much kings suck

Now let's put those two words from above together. A country has a "direct democracy" when its people get to vote on what's important to them, in the most direct way possible, with nothing standing in the way.

What could stand in the way? Well, to be honest, it's usually other people.

Other kinds of democracies:

Representative democracy

Presidential democracy

Authoritarian democracy

Others

The important thing to remember is that most countries have representative democracy, not direct democracy. Wild and wacky Switzerland breaks the mold and blends both together...and it works.

The very cool thing about Switzerland's form of democracy is everybody—and I mean everybody—can suggest new laws or suggest changes to existing laws. If people vote on a law the government has passed, it's called a "referendum." If a Swiss citizen—or a group of citizens—make the suggestions themselves, it's called a "popular initiative"...and it's very popular indeed.

Popular initiative

The Swiss vote on everything—and I mean everything! Ballots are sent out to all voters four times per year. The dates for voting are already decided all the way through 2038. These are people who love to vote!

Besides voting on the regular stuff that's proposed by the government, the people of Switzerland themselves came up with 192 popular initiatives between 1893 and 2014. That is no small task.

So, you think you have an idea for a new law? You've got some work ahead of you.

Let's imagine your initiative is that all Swiss people should HAVE TO eat ice cream on Sundays.

OK, now here's what you need to do:

1. Set up an Initiative Committee of between seven and twenty-seven citizens. Make sure they like each other…and also love ice cream.

Erdbeere   Fraise   Fragola

ICE CREAM

2. Write your initiative in one of the national languages (German, French, or Italian). Imagine writing a very long school essay with up to twenty-seven people arguing about what goes into it. Easy peasy.

3. If you've gotten this far, the government then allows you eighteen months to collect 100,000 signatures from other citizens who also want to force everyone to eat ice cream every Sunday. Think that's easy? Think again.

4. All 100,000 signatures must come from Swiss citizens
who have the right to vote. So, no ice cream-loving outsiders allowed.

5. Realize that the government will probably send information to all voters
explaining why they should NOT eat ice cream on Sundays.

6. Be prepared to wait up to five years to see your Ice Cream Initiative
on the ballot. Hope you're not in a hurry.

So, how did it turn out for those 192 proposed popular initiatives, you ask?

Ninety-seven of them were rejected by voters or not allowed by the government for various reasons.

Seventy-three were withdrawn by the people proposing them.

Of the rest, only twenty-two were voted into official Swiss law. 'Only twenty-two?' you groan. Well, yeah. But that's twenty-two times that Swiss voters had their voices directly heard.

Most initiatives have nothing to do with ice cream. OK, in fact, none of them did. They were about healthcare, taxes, welfare, drug policies, public transportation, immigration, or education. But there have been a few "quirky" ones, as well. See if you can pick them out below...

True or False? (answers below)

- The first successful popular initiative passed in 1893, making it illegal to SLAUGHTER ANIMALS WITHOUT KNOCKING THEM OUT WITH ANESTHESIA. No more sneaking up behind a pig and bopping him on the head!
- Exactly one hundred years later, in 1993, another popular initiative turned the 1st of August into a national holiday. The entire population of Switzerland could finally take a day off work and school to shoot off fireworks, light bonfires, and bop pigs on the head (after putting them to sleep, of course) so they could turn them into the several million cervelats (the nation's favorite sausage) to be roasted over the coals of the fires.
- An initiative designed to give all Swiss people six weeks of vacation (instead of only four weeks) was proposed in 2012. Unbelievably, all twenty-six cantons turned it down, leaving most of the rest of the world scratching its head. Seriously? Who votes against vacation?

- In 1978, the country voted on whether or not to adopt Daylight Savings Time. That's when the clocks are moved forward by one hour in spring and backwards by one hour in autumn to give people more daylight. The Swiss voters turned it down, some arguing that the change would "confuse the cows" by disrupting their milking schedules. The government decided to use Daylight Savings Time anyway. There are rumors that the cows are still planning to fight the decision with an initiative of their own...

Fooled you! All of the above are true!

Ridiculous, but true

Swiss women didn't have the right to vote in any national elections until 1971. The idea had been proposed—and rejected—in 1959, but supporters kept arguing and protesting until it became law.

Even though women won the right to vote in national elections in 1971, the half-cantons of Appenzell Ausserrhoden and Appenzell Innerrhoden still wouldn't let women vote in local elections. The Supreme Court of Switzerland decided to step in and—by 1990—all Swiss women had the right to vote in all elections.

Strangely enough, the main reason for the delay in granting democratic rights to women was the system of direct democracy itself. Once the initiative for giving women voting rights made it onto the ballot, the majority of MALE voters in every canton had to actually vote for it. Any questions?

Speaking in Tongues

English	Swiss German	French
A. Hello	A. Grüezi	A. Bonjour
B. Head	B. Chopf	B. Tête
C. Brain	C. Hirni	C. Cerveau
D. Mouth	D. Muul	D. Bouche
E. Bottom	E. Füdli	E. Fesses
F. Burp	F. Gorbse	F. Rot
G. Crumbs	G. Brösmeli	G. Les miettes
H. Little Fart	H. Furzli	H. Petit pet
I. Stinky feet	I. Chäsfüess	I. Pieds puants

Italian	Romansh
A. Ciao	A. allegra
B. Testa	B. chau
C. Cervello	C. tscharvè
D. Bocca	D. bocca
E. Natiche	E. chül
F. Rutto	F. rupch
G. Briciole	G. miclas
H. Piccolo scoreggia	H. tof
I. Piedi puzzolenti	I. pês chi spüzzan da chaschöl

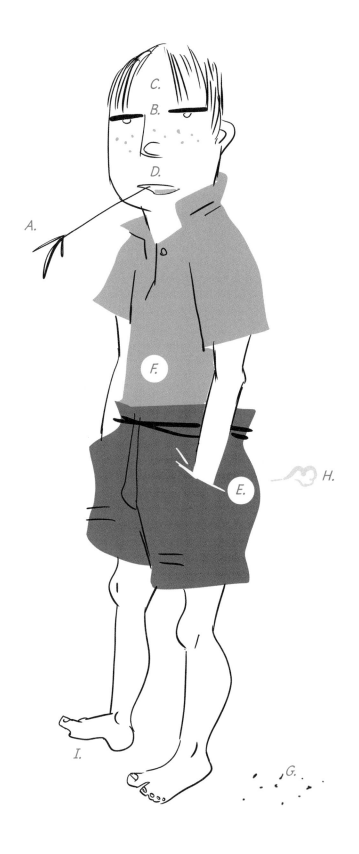

Languages of Switzerland

Switzerland is a collection of twenty-six cantons that joined the country at one point or another in history. By 1815, Switzerland's wonky borders we all know and love were defined. The result is a mishmash of different peoples speaking four different languages—plus countless dialects—with significantly different cultures. But they all identify themselves as Swiss.

Most of the Swiss speak German as their main language... a whopping 63% of the population. It's understandable that the other language groups feel outnumbered and overwhelmed at times. Only 23% of the population speak French, 8.2% speak Italian, and a tiny 0.5% speak Romansh. So, you can expect some hard feelings between the groups from time to time.

Who speaks what, where?

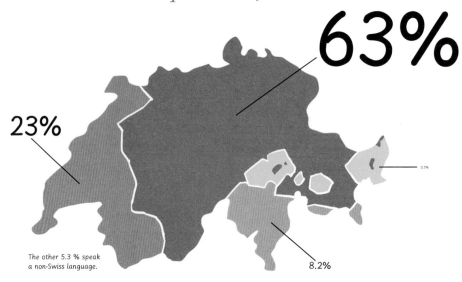

63%

23%

0.5%

The other 5.3 % speak
a non-Swiss language.

8.2%

Yes, there's a bit of grumbling, and plenty of jokes about the "others." But it actually all works out fairly well. Except when it doesn't. So how do the Swiss let off some steam about the "others" in the country?

Well, believe it or not, they often take it out on license plates. Each license plate number starts with an abbreviation for the canton where the car is registered. So a car from Zurich will have a number that starts with ZH. The license plate for a car from Uri will start with UR. And so on.

A running joke among many people in Switzerland has to do with the abbreviations on each license plate. Angry with a driver from Aargau? Think of him/her by the unofficial AG abbreviation on his license plate and feel better. Here are some examples (in Swiss German, Zurich dialect):

1. Zurich – ZH – *Zwenig Hirni* = Too little brains
2. Bern – BE – *Bin igschlafe* = I fell asleep
3. Luzern – LU – *Löli unterwägs* = Idiot on the road
4. Uri – UR – *Unfähige Raser* = Incompetent speeder
5. Schwyz – SZ – *Schweine-Züchter* = Pig breeder
6. Obwalden – OW – *Ohne Wort* = Speechless
7. Nidwalden – NW – *Nüd-Wüsser* = Know-nothing
8. Glarus – GL – *Ghirnlos* = Without a brain
9. Zug – ZG – *Zuedröhnt* = Totally drunk
10. Freiburg - FR – *fahrender Rambos* = Driving Rambos
11. Solothurn – SO – *Soiniggel* = Disgusting person
12. Basel-Stadt – BS – *Bald Schrott* = Soon to be wreckage
13. Basel-Landschaft – BL – *Blöder Lulatsch* = Stupid beanpole
14. Schaffhausen – SH – *Sauhund* = Bloody swine
15. Appenzell Ausserrhoden – AR = *Altä Raser* = Old speeder
16. Appenzell Innerrhoden – AI = *Altä Idiot* = Old idiot
17. St. Gallen – SG – *Sonaglööwn* = Such a clown
18. Graubunden – GR – *Gebirgs Raser* = Mountain speeder
19. Aargau – AG – *Achtung, Gfahr!* = Be careful, danger!
20. Thurgau – TG – *Taube Glööwn* = Deaf clown
21. Ticino – TI – *Totaler Idiot* = Total idiot
22. Vaud – VD – *Völlig doof* = Totally stupid
23. Wallis – VS – *Völlig scheisse* = Totally crap
24. Neuchatel – NE – *Nöd ischlafe* = Don't fall asleep
25. Genf – GE – *Gstörte Eselstriber* = Disturbed donkey driver
26. Jura – JU – *Junge Unruhestifter* = Young troublemaker

Achtung, Gfahr!

Zwenig Hirni

Unfähige Raser

These are only examples...and probably some of the more polite ones! There are bound to be many ruder versions.

If you've heard Swiss French or Swiss Italian being spoken, you might have noticed that they're pretty close to the languages spoken in France and Italy. Sure, there are a few variations, but nothing too major. Swiss German, however, is usually a puzzle to most Germans unless they live near the border of Switzerland.

How Swiss German sounds to Germans

Could you tell me the way to the Matterhorn?

Iu. Horu.

Uhhh, I'm not quite sure I understand!

Äbedeschogäuhautimmerahi.

Matterhorn?

Moudescho.

Well...thank you anyway.

Ade.

Swiss German name generator

Have some fun in Swiss German (in this case with the Zurich dialect). Take the first letter of your first name and replace it with the matching word in the left column. Then do the same with your last name and the right column. See what you get.

Examples:

Laurie Theurer would be *Chützeligs Hüehnli* or "Ticklish Hen".

Justin Bieber would be *Agfurzts Tomätli* or "Farted-on Tomato".

A	Blöds (stupid)		A	Müüsli (mouse)
B	Riisigs (giant)		B	Tomätli (tomato)
C	Chotzigs (barfy)		C	Chueli (cow)
D	Fuuls (lazy)		D	Tubbeli (moron)
E	Halbschlaus (half clever)		E	Eseli (donkey)
F	Schnuderigs (snotty)		F	Rüebli (carrot)
G	Erbrochnigs (barfed up)		G	Büebli (boy)
H	Chliises (small)		H	Geissli (goat)
I	Dumms (dumb)		I	Löffeli (spoon)
J	Agfurzts (farted on)		J	Tüüfeli (devil)
K	Luschigts (funny)		K	Hundli (dog)
L	Chützeligs (ticklish)		L	Chäferli (beetle)
M	Grusigs (disgusting)		M	Eili (egg)

N	Früündlichs (friendly)		N	Chuchichäschtli (kitchen cabinet)
O	Bösi (nasty)		O	Lööli (bozo)
P	Gfrornigs (frozen)		P	Säuli (piglet)
Q	Gmüetlichs (cozy)		Q	Znüni (morning snack)
R	Stinkigs (stinky)		R	Bibeli (baby chick)
S	Müeds (tired)		S	Banänli (banana)
T	Abislets (peed on)		T	Hüehnli (hen)
U	Gfürchigs (creepy)		U	Abfallsäckli (trash bag)
V	Schöns (beautiful)		V	Bettmümpfeli (bedtime snack)
W	Schüchs (timid)		W	Chatzli (cat)
X	Agwiderets (disgusting)		X	Chüechli (cake)
Y	Doofs (stupid)		Y	Büggeli (bumps)
Z	Fürchterlichs (terrible)		Z	Würmli (worm)

Industrious

Eight things the Swiss didn't have before industrialization

Devices to make life easier

Railroads

Fast food

Chocolate bars

Industrialists

Child labor in factories

Hydroelectric power

Awesome machines to
make kids work faster

Chemical factories

Switzerland was one of the first industrialized countries. This means that, back in the 1800s, the Swiss were one of the first nations to build factories and use machinery to make stuff or to get stuff done. What kind of stuff? The kind of stuff that made people's lives—and yours today—easier, better, and more convenient.

"So, what does that have to do with me exactly?" you ask. Take a look around you…

Most everything you wear, eat, or ride around in (or on) was made in some sort of factory

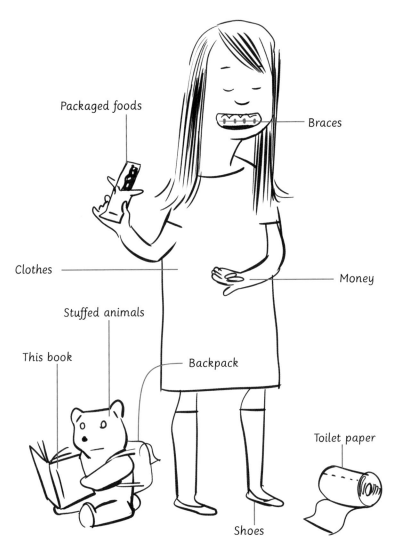

Packaged foods

Braces

Clothes

Money

Stuffed animals

This book

Backpack

Toilet paper

Shoes

Before the Industrial Revolution, people had to make everything by hand. Clothing, shoes, houses, food...everything! If you didn't make it yourself—or buy it from someone else who had made it themselves—then you didn't have it.

When "it" becomes too much of a good thing

The British led the way to industrialization in Europe. They had colonies all over the world where they could get raw materials and ship them home. They also had great trading relationships with lots of other countries, so they could get all the raw materials they needed if their colonies didn't have them. Put that together with their huge supplies of coal that powered their machines, and you can see why Great Britain became an industrial power-house during the 18th and 19th centuries.

Why England was richer

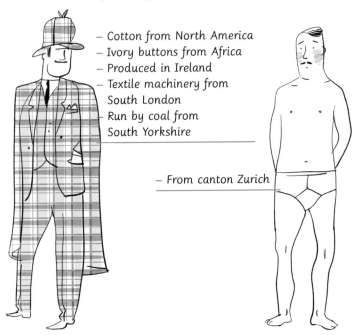

- Cotton from North America
- Ivory buttons from Africa
- Produced in Ireland
- Textile machinery from South London
- Run by coal from South Yorkshire

- From canton Zurich

Industry-wise, Switzerland followed closely behind Great Britain...but Switzerland didn't have colonies, didn't have much coal to dig up and burn, and didn't have the right natural resources to make much of anything in factories. When you get right down to it, Switzerland never had any of the "normal" stuff needed to succeed in the Industrial Age.

Switzerland's major natural resources

Granite and limestone

Salt

Forests

What Switzerland did have was more important...people with a strong work ethic and the ability to innovate—and a bit of dumb luck.

Take textiles, for example. Up until 1800, Switzerland had what was called a cottage industry.

"Cottage industry" basically means that products were made in people's homes, rather than in a factory. At the time, there were plenty of farming families in Switzerland earning extra money by making things, like wool cloth and embroidery, working at home. Industrialization changed all that.

The first textile machines were made in Great Britain in 1764 and, suddenly, textiles could be produced faster and more cheaply by machines than by hand. Swiss companies imported some of these machines from Great Britain and never looked back.

The first mechanical spinning mills using British machinery opened in St. Gallen in 1801 and in Zurich in 1802...and Switzerland was on its way. Here's where the dumb luck came into play, too.

In the first years of the 1800s, Napoleon's soldiers still occupied Switzerland while he was continuing to invade, attack, and conquer all over Europe. One of the few countries Napoleon hadn't "collected" yet was Great Britain...and he wanted it really, really badly.

Napoleonic temper tantrum

In order to make Great Britain easier to defeat, Napoleon set up the Continental Blockade in 1806. Basically, it prohibited all European ports from trading goods with Great Britain, which meant British businesses wouldn't be able to earn money. Napoleon thought that if he caused Great Britain's economic collapse, it would be easier to invade and conquer it afterwards.

Napoleon the bully

After six years of success, Napoleon's plan backfired. When he pushed Russia too hard about the blockade, and then invaded it to make his point in 1812, he made one of the biggest military blunders in history and got his butt solidly kicked in the process. Blockade over. Then he got his butt kicked one last time at Waterloo in 1815. Napoleon was sent into exile until his miserable death in 1821. Ooopsies.

But for Switzerland, the six years of Napoleon's Continental Blockade were a blessing in disguise. British cotton and textiles were suddenly not available anymore. Somebody needed to fill the gap...why not the Swiss? Also, when the Swiss found they could no longer import British textile machinery, they were forced to try to produce their own. Turns out the Swiss were really good at it. Who knew?

Also, as it turned out, the Swiss didn't need to rely on filthy coal to power their machinery because they had something Great Britain lacked...mountains gushing with flowing water. They figured out how to harness the waters' energy and used it to power their factories. Very cool, no?

So now the Swiss were experts at inventing and producing machinery, and they had the resources they needed to power those machines cleanly and efficiently. Business was booming. Income was increasing. Things were looking good.

Industrialization in Switzerland was about to go hypersonic. The more textile factories there were, the more people wanted new colors and dyes for their fabrics. You don't want to just wear beige all the time, do you? New dye-making chemical factories popped up along the Rhine river in Basel, as you need lots of water to make colors and dyes.

And that was just the beginning. The big money in chemicals isn't in giving people pretty clothes, but in helping sick people get healthy again.

What do you do when you're sick? Barf? Maybe. Sniff, sneeze, and cough? Probably. Take medicine to make yourself feel better? Probably not before industrialization because there weren't that many medicines around compared to today. Did you know that many of the medicines we commonly use today wouldn't be around if industrialization had never reached Basel—which is one of the pharmaceutical centers of the world?

Watchmaking had been big in Switzerland since the 1500s, but now with new and improved machinery, as well as access to more and more raw metals, that boomed as well. By 1850, the Swiss were making over two million watches per year. What would the world be without massively expensive Swiss watches? Or the ultra-fashionable Swatch?

Until the 1840s, there was really no railway system to speak of in Switzerland. A man named Alfred Escher changed all that. After returning from a six-month trip to Paris in 1843, he realized that Switzerland was far behind the rest of Europe and was hurting itself by not developing a railway system. Trains would bring materials from factory to factory, people from city to city, and boost the overall economy of the country. Escher made a plan and pushed it through, setting-up railway lines and tunnels all over Switzerland. He also started the first major Swiss bank, which helped to pay for these railway lines...it's now known as Credit Suisse, today one of the world's biggest banks. By 1864, Escher had helped to increase the rail network in Switzerland from 38 kilometers to 1300 kilometers of rails. Not too shabby, eh? In 1898, the Swiss government decided to buy the five largest railway companies. The Swiss Federal Railways (SBB) was founded in 1902.

Switzerland as a whole was booming. Industry was thriving. Life was sweet...but not for everybody.

Industrialization had a dark side.

While company owners got richer and richer, their workers were earning money, but they were also working longer and longer hours to earn it. There were no laws at the time about how many hours a person should work per day. There was no such thing as vacation days or sick leave. Perhaps worst of them all...there was no law that said how old workers had to be in order to work. In fact, child labor was totally normal.

Before labor laws were invented

Marie, be back to work on Monday. The kid starts on Tuesday.

In the past, Swiss kids were always expected to help out on the farm, in the workshop, or in the home, according to their age and abilities. Once industrialization rolled around, this didn't change. Parents still expected their kids to help—except now it got much, much worse for the kids.

As more and more factories sprang up, the need for laborers became greater and greater. Kids were forced to work equally long hours as their parents and had little or no protections, such as safety gear, rest periods, or even the opportunity to go to school. In the textile factories that sprang up along the Aabach River east of Zurich, about one third of the factory workers were under the age of sixteen. Kids whose parents had looms or embroidery machines at home worked there every day, as well. Playtime? Forget it, kid.

Kids, with their little fingers and ability to scamper around underneath the textile machines, were used in textile factories to change spindles of thread.

It was dangerous work, and many of them lost hands or fingers in the machinery

It took some time, but there was finally an outcry about the working conditions for children. Inspectors noticed the children's hunched backs, damaged eyesight, and general exhaustion. Laws were put into place, such as...

1815: Zurich

"Regulation of underage youth in general and regarding spinning machines especially."

This regulation stated that kids nine years old or older could only work at spinning machines for fourteen hours per day, instead of the usual sixteen hours per day. Whoopee! Two hours less, right? Too bad these regulations were never enforced. Kids worked just as long and hard as ever. But it was a start.

1837: Zurich

The Great Council of Zurich issued a regulation on child labor and prohibited the employment of school-age children in factories. Too bad it didn't regulate child labor anywhere else. But it was progress.

1842: Aargau

The parliament decided not to limit the hours of child labor. Big step backwards.

1846: Glarus

Reduction on the length of work to 15 hours per day for adults and 14 hours per day for children under 14. Another (small) step forwards.

1858: Glarus

Ban on work on Sundays for everyone. Huge step forwards!

1864: Glarus

Reduction of the length of work to 12 hours, a total ban on night work for everyone (8pm to 5am) and a prohibition of work for children under the age of 12. New mothers were entitled to six weeks off after giving birth.

1872: Glarus

Maximum work day of eleven hours for everyone. Another step forwards.

1877: All of Switzerland

The Switzerland-wide "Federal Factory Act" regulated factory work for the first time in all of Switzerland and completely replaced the regulations of the individual cantons. Based on the factory act of 1872 in Glarus, kids under fourteen were not allowed to even set foot in factories. It was good in theory, but in reality it didn't really work out so well. The regulation did not state, for example, that children couldn't be forced to work elsewhere. Bummer. Many factories decided to increase the amount of work that could be done at home...meaning that kids of all ages could be kept slaving away at all hours in their own cellars. In addition to that, the new law stated that all children MUST go to school. This meant that children were expected to go to school *and* work long hours... often deep into the night. In many cases where children were still working illegally in factories—and it happened—they were often so exhausted that their parents or siblings had to carry them to work while they were still sleeping so they could get an early morning start before school.

Typical day for a factory kid in Switzerland

5:30am: work

8:00am: go to school (after a few cups of coffee)

12:00pm: lunch (or no lunch...depending...)

12:15pm: work

1:00pm: back to school

4:00pm: work

7:30pm: dinner (with a few more cups of coffee)

8:00pm: work into the night

Rest of the night: Mostly awake (due to a few too many cups of coffee)

But overwork wasn't the only danger. Average life expectancy for people in factories was only 35 years.

Nasty ways to die in factories

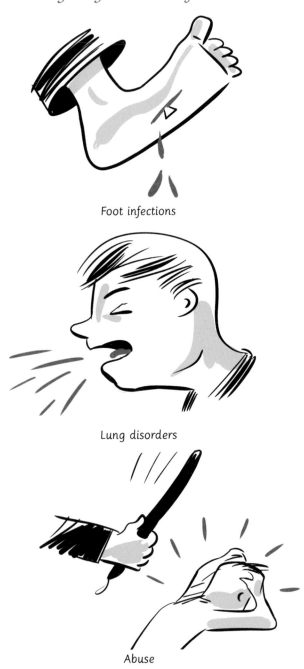

Foot infections

Lung disorders

Abuse

Even after the passing of the 1877 law, it took about 20 more years until all factory owners actually paid attention to it.

Finally! No more child labor!! Except at home...

Mountain

Beginning of time–1555

1555–1864

The Evolution of Mountaineering

Madness

1864–Present

Future

Since the beginning of time, mountains have been a source of wonder—and terror—for people in Switzerland. As late as the 1800s, most Swiss people wouldn't have dared to venture too high up any mountain...not even on a dare.

That all changed in Switzerland during the 1850s—and it had a lot to do with wealthy British people and the Industrial Revolution.

Wait. What? What do rich Brits, machines, and factories have to do with how the Swiss felt about their mountains?

During the Industrial Revolution, work that people used to do by hand could suddenly be done by machines. That caused a shift in how people worked and how many hours they needed to work. It also made many people very, very rich. The industrial revolution came to England earlier than it did to Switzerland. So those rich Brits had time and money on their hands. Time for the next challenge.

Climbing in Britain was not challenging enough

England is a country without really tall mountains, so unless people wanted the challenge of climbing the nearest rolling green hillside, they had to look for something more exciting. Enter Switzerland with its lots, and lots (and lots) of mountains just waiting to be conquered.

Up until that time, the farmers in Switzerland knew the mountain trails well—at least those that would let their livestock graze sweet grass in the mountain meadows—and the best places to hunt.

When it's good to be a domesticated animal

Suddenly, tons of explorers from Britain wanted to climb the Swiss mountains…and they wanted to be the first to get to the top, each and every time. Hungry for glory, they were ready to throw lots of money at the people most knowledgeable about the Swiss mountains—the Swiss farmers and hunters—and hire them as guides. The race for British glory (and Swiss mountain guide income) was officially on. The Swiss weren't about to turn their backs on that kind of cash. Suddenly, the mountain peaks were no longer so scary. Swiss farmers and hunters clambered to bring the Brits to the top. And naturalists ventured higher and higher in the interests of science.

The Golden Age of Mountaineering

Alfred Wills was a successful judge for England and Wales who was also crazy about mountain climbing…and had the money to do it. He hired two Swiss chamois hunters to help him reach the top of the Wetterhorn in 1854. Of course, the chamois hunters jumped at the chance to earn some extra money, so they rebranded themselves as mountain guides and off they went with Wills up the Wetterhorn. They helped Wills reach the top, all the while "forgetting" to tell him that Johann Jaun and Melchior Bannholzer had already climbed to the top of the Wetterhorn ten years earlier.

They got their income and Wills got the glory. Everybody happy.

After news got out about Wills conquering the Wetterhorn, lots of other people all over the world wanted to outdo them. Over the next ten years, dozens of Alpine peaks were summited by adventurers and their Swiss guides. The adventurers wrote lots and lots (and lots) of books about their feats of manliness. The Swiss guides, unfortunately, did not write much about mountaineering back then. They were too busy guiding adventurers up and down the mountains.

Swiss guide earning a living

Up and down:
100 Francs
Up only:
10 Francs

The end of the Golden Age of Mountaineering

A young British adventurer named Edward Whymper led the first successful ascent of the Matterhorn in 1865. It was one of the last Swiss peaks that had not yet been conquered. Whymper and a few other climbers hired some local guides and made their way up the Swiss side of the mountain. They hoped to reach the top before another team of climbers, who had just started up the Italian side. It was truly a race to the top.

Whymper and his team made it to the summit with a short time to spare. They celebrated a bit before looking down and seeing the Italian team only about 400 meters below them. Whymper and his men wanted to be sure that the other team knew that they had lost the race, so they shouted down the mountain at them and kicked stones onto their heads. The men in the other team scrambled in panic back down the way they had come.

Clearly, sportsmanship was not part of the glory of the climb.

Scorecard		
Points for:	Other team	Whymper's team
Reaching the top	0	1
Sportsmanship	1	0
Lives about to be lost	0	4

If Wills' climb up the Wetterhorn marked the beginning of the Golden Age of Moutaineering, Whymper's descent of the Matterhorn definitely marked the end of it. Whymper had included a very inexperienced man on his team of seven climbers. On the way down, this inexperienced man slipped and pulled three men on the same rope off their feet. The rope connecting them to Whymper and the other two men snapped. So four unlucky men fell to their deaths while Whymper and two guides did not. An inspection of the rope determined that it was of poor quality and should not have been used except as an emergency back up. Whymper, as leader of the expedition, didn't want to accept full blame for the tragedy. Glory above all else, right?

Before

After

So, you might say that The Golden Age of Mountaineering didn't go out with a bang...but rather with a Whymper.

Following Whymper's tragedy on the Matterhorn, Queen Victoria very nearly banned mountaineering in Switzerland for all people from Great Britain. It wouldn't have mattered, though. By that time, most of the peaks in Switzerland had already been conquered. Been there. Done that. Those who wanted to be the first to climb new peaks had to look further away to the Caucasus, the Andes, the Rockies, and the Himalayas. But Whymper's disastrous climb had put Switzerland "on the map." Tourists now wanted to see it for themselves. By the 1900s, Switzerland was full of hikers and climbers in the summer and, by the middle of the 20th century, skiers in the winter. The mountain regions in Switzerland were transformed from poor, rural areas into true international tourist destinations. Just like that.

The women whose accomplishments were ignored during the Golden Age of Mountaineering

Seriously? You weren't planning on ending the chapter without writing about us, were you? WERE YOU?

You won't find many details about women climbers during the Golden Age of Mountaineering as—unlike the men—the leading female climbers during this period were more into climbing than glorifying their achievements in books. The men, on the other hand, spent a LOT of time writing about themselves and their adventures. No time for wasting words on girl climbers.

Women were up there, though. In the Swiss mountain wilderness. Much more than anyone suspected.

Lucy Walker (1836–1916)

When Lucy Walker was twenty, she had painful rheumatism that made her joints swollen and stiff. Her doctor advised her to walk as much as possible, so that's exactly what she did. Her father and brother were already regularly climbing mountains in Switzerland, so Lucy decided to join them. You might think that's no big deal these days, but such a thing was unheard of for a woman in the Britain of 1856! Lucy Walker was the first woman to regularly climb in the Alps and the first woman to summit many of its peaks. Her climbing career spanned twenty-one years and included ninety-eight different summits. Here's the kicker...she refused to dress in men's climbing attire, and there were no climbing clothes or boots for women.

Lucy Walker's climbing attire in 1856

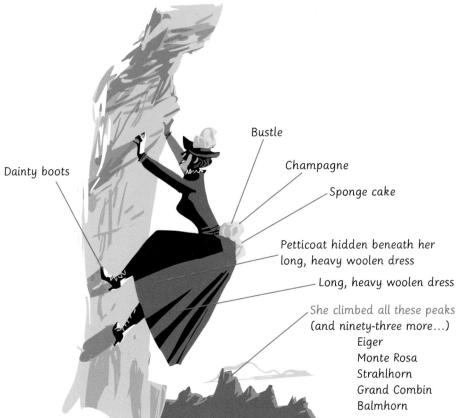

Bustle

Champagne

Sponge cake

Dainty boots

Petticoat hidden beneath her long, heavy woolen dress

Long, heavy woolen dress

She climbed all these peaks (and ninety-three more...)
Eiger
Monte Rosa
Strahlhorn
Grand Combin
Balmhorn

Even with all her heavy, constricting clothing and dainty boots, Lucy Walker out-climbed many of the male members of the British Alpine Club...the same club that would not let her join as she was not a man. So naturally, she joined—and then became president of—the Ladies Alpine Club. And she kept setting new records.

Meta Brevoort (1825-1876)

One of Lucy Walker's biggest climbing rivals was Meta Brevoort, an American woman who only started climbing mountains at the age of forty. A powerhouse of a woman, she went from the luxury of a convent school education in Paris to scrambling around the mountains of Switzerland. She's famous for being the first woman to dare to wear men's trousers while climbing, although she wouldn't let anyone photograph her wearing them.

Brevoort's greatest ambition was to be the first woman to stand atop the Matterhorn. Unfortunately, Lucy Walker heard of Brevoort's plans and rushed to beat her there. Walker was standing on top of the Matterhorn a few days before Brevoort could even get started up the mountain with her team. Brevoort didn't let that get her down, though, and went on to set many records of her own.

Brevoort took her young nephew, W.A.B. Coolidge, with her on many, many climbs. He went on to become one of the best-known climbers during The Silver Age of Mountaineering (after The Golden Age of Mountaineering ended with a Whymper). Their favorite Swiss guide—Christian Almer—gave W.A.B. Coolidge a beagle as a gift during one of their climbing trips. The three (Brevoort, Coolidge, and Tschingel the dog) became known as "the most famous trio in the alps." In 1875, the dog was elected as an honorary member of the Alpine Club, even though she was a female dog. But Brevoort?

A female human? Not a chance.

WORLD

Europe 1939
The "Before" shot*
(*Every country going about its own business)

WAR II

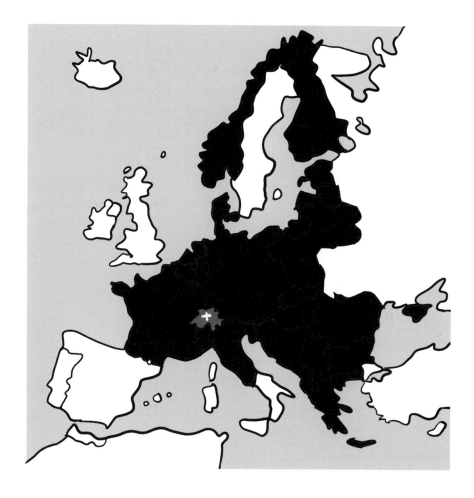

Europe 1944
The "After" shot*
(*See that little splotch of red in the middle of Nazi-occupied black?
Yep, that's Switzerland…completely surrounded…)

On September 1st, 1939, the leader of Nazi Germany—Adolf Hitler—invaded neighboring Poland. Hitler had been big trouble ever since becoming chancellor of Germany in 1933. He'd established a totalitarian regime, meaning that everybody had to do what he said…and what he was saying was pretty awful. He defined what a proper German person should look like and what they should believe. He also wanted to "cleanse" the rest of Europe so only the "proper" people were left. Life became difficult for everyone else, especially for people who were Jewish.

Switzerland watched Hitler's actions closely. He'd attacked Poland without warning. Who knew what Hitler would do next… and to which neighbor? Switzerland—as a tiny country with a limited army right next to enormous, powerful Germany—was particularly worried.

German Domination vs. Swiss Limitation during WWII

Swiss Limitation	German Domination
Population: 4,226,000	Population: 69,838,000
Military troops: 850,000	Military troops: 18,000,000
Artillery: Not so much	Artillery: Lots and lots

Nazi Germany, and its allies Japan and Italy, were known as the Axis powers. As feared, they went on to invade most of mainland Europe, the Middle East, Northern Africa and Southeast Asia. Lots of other countries fought back against the Axis Powers, including France, Great Britain, Australia, New Zealand, Canada, South Africa and eventually the Soviet Union and the United States. They were known as the Allies. Countries including Switzerland, Spain, Portugal, and Sweden held back and waited to see what would happen. They were called the Neutral Countries.

Hitler's grand vision was of a "New World Order," with Germany leading all of Europe, and Japan leading most of Asia.

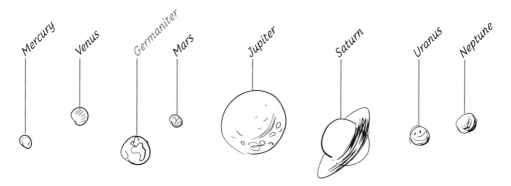

Mercury   Venus   Germaniter   Mars   Jupiter   Saturn   Uranus   Neptune

Luckily, Hitler's plan didn't work out the way he wanted. After six years of war, the Allies were victorious. It was an expensive war, though, both financially and in the cost of human lives—the deadliest war in history.

It's estimated that 70–85 million people died worldwide as a result of World War II...which was about 3% of the world population at that time. A majority of the dead, 50–56 million, were either soldiers in battle or civilians who were too close to the battles. The remaining 19–28 million died from war-related diseases or starvation.

So, what about the Swiss? What was going on in Switzerland during those grueling years of war?

Believe it or not, only about 100 people in Switzerland died as a result of World War II battles. Most of them due to mistakes on the part of Allied airmen. More on that below. Even surrounded as it was by war and under constant threat of invasion by Nazi Germany...Switzerland went relatively untouched. But that doesn't mean that things weren't tense.

Armed Neutrality

Switzerland saw the war coming. Two days before Germany invaded Poland, the Swiss Federal Assembly elected former-farmer-turned-General Henri Guisan to lead their troops and try to keep Switzerland safe.

On the day before the invasion, Switzerland sent out a message of neutrality to forty countries, declaring that the Swiss were unwilling to fight in any war.

The day of the invasion of Poland, General Guisan called for all Swiss troops to be ready to defend Switzerland. Within forty-eight hours, 430,000 Swiss troops were armed and in position. Local guards and veterans joined the call, bringing Switzerland's protective forces to over 850,000…not bad for a country with a population of only about four million people at the time.

Answering the call

Was that enough to fully protect Switzerland and its citizens from the gigantic German war machine? Nope. General Guisan and his troops knew that well enough. In mid-June 1940, Switzerland only had 24 reconnaissance tanks, 90 war-ready fighter planes, and 60,000 horses...definitely not enough to fight back against one of the deadliest armies ever.

So, as the war went on into 1940, and the Axis Powers conquered more and more of Europe, Guisan came up with a plan. He called 650 of his top officers to meet at the Rütli Meadow—the legendary site of the Rütli Oath and the supposed birthplace of Switzerland.

There he told them about the dangers facing Switzerland, the likelihood that it would be invaded, his desire to resist at all costs, and how he could see that happening

The Swiss National Redoubt was a plan that had been put into place by the Swiss government in the 1880s in case of foreign invasion. The idea was to secure the mountainous central part of Switzerland by providing a place for the Swiss army to retreat during an invasion. From there, they could fight back against the intruders using the supplies stored there.

General Guisan's plan was to expand the National Redoubt. Within months, the Swiss army stocked fortifications in the mountains with supplies, artillery, and 360,000 soldiers (half the Swiss army itself), spending 90 million Swiss francs to ensure they were ready to face and destroy any potential invaders.

They also loaded alpine roads, railway lines, and tunnels with massive amounts of explosives, ready to blow them up at a moment's notice to stop invading troops if needed.

Doing so would also destroy transport lines between Germany and Italy, leaving them cut off from each other and without many of the materials they would need to continue their attack against Switzerland.

General Guisan made absolutely sure that the Axis Powers knew all about the National Redoubt. Switzerland never was invaded during World War II, and Hitler's knowledge of the National Redoubt probably had a lot to do with that.

The best offense is a good defense

Even when completely surrounded by Axis Powers, Switzerland pulled together its troops and prepared for the worst...without freaking out. German troops tried many times to taunt Swiss soldiers by crossing Switzerland's northern border or by flying over Swiss airspace, but the Swiss managed to keep calm and didn't let their soldiers react.

During the Battle of France, German aircraft violated Swiss airspace no fewer than 197 times. Although the Swiss did not participate in the battles themselves, they did shoot down eleven German planes that had flown into Swiss airspace between May and June 1940. This infuriated Hitler, so Germany lodged a diplomatic protest. As a result, the Swiss Air Force was ordered to stop intercepting planes that strayed into their airspace. So the Swiss pilots came up with another idea. Instead of shooting German planes down, they instead forced intruders to land at Swiss airports and airfields. Once on the ground, the German planes and their pilots would be in neutral Swiss territory and could be detained for the duration of the war. Needless to say, Hitler was not happy about that either.

In fact, Hitler sent saboteurs to destroy Swiss airfields, but the Swiss troops captured them before they could cause any damage

The Germans were not the only pilots to violate Swiss airspace, though. Let's face it... when flying over central Europe, it's kind of hard to avoid Switzerland. In fact, during the entire length of the war, it's estimated that 6304 Allied aircraft violated Swiss airspace.

The Swiss didn't freak out about these events until tragedy struck...a few times. In April 1944, an American plane dropped bombs on Schaffhausen, mistaking it for Ludwigshafen am Rhein (a German town 284 kilometers away). Then, in February 1945, confused Allied airmen bombed Stein am Rhein, Vals, and Rafz. The pilots' confusion led to the bombing of Basel and Zurich in March 1945.

The pilots responsible for the Zurich bombing mistook it for Freiburg, Germany

These incidents accounted for most of the 100 Swiss people killed during World War II we talked about earlier. The Swiss considered these incidents as "accidents" but also made it clear that—from that point forward—single aircraft caught straying into Swiss airspace would be forced down and their crews kept in Swiss internment camps until the end of the war. Any aircraft flying in bomber formation over Switzerland would be intercepted and shot down...no matter if they were Allied or Axis planes.

The Cultivation Battle

During any war, food supplies are limited. The Swiss realized this was true, even though they had no plans to be actively involved in the war. Before the war, about 50% of food in Switzerland was imported from other countries in Europe. The Swiss knew that there was a good chance that those supplies would get cut off when war was underway. So, the ever-practical Swiss government ordered the planting of every available plot of land with grains, vegetables, and potatoes to ensure they could feed themselves during the war years. They called it the "Cultivation Battle." Every available private and public bit of earth was planted, including patches at private homes, schools, soccer fields, and even the front lawn of a library or two.

By the end of World War II, the amount of cultivated soil in Switzerland had tripled, meaning that Switzerland only had to import about 20% of its food from other countries during that time.

Refugees

Bad news at the Swiss border

In order to keep its neutral and free status, Switzerland had to make many difficult decisions before and during World War II. People have many opinions about whether these decisions were right or wrong, and whether these decisions were "neutral" enough.

During World War II, Hitler ordered the murder of six million people, simply because they were Jewish. That was about two thirds of the Jewish population of Europe. He ordered the murder of millions more. Many people—Jewish or not—had to flee. Lots of people, including those in Switzerland, did their best to help these refugees. Tiny Switzerland took in about 300,000 refugees and let thousands more pass through Switzerland on their way to safety elsewhere.

Things changed, though, when Germany threatened to invade Switzerland itself. In 1942, in order to avoid angering Hitler any further, Switzerland started refusing entry to refugees at the border. This meant that thousands of people were turned away and sent back into Nazi Germany. If they happened to be Jewish, they were almost certainly being sent to their deaths.

Money. Business as usual...and unusual business

Before the war, the Swiss had trade agreements with many European countries. They bought things that were not available in Switzerland and sold things that were. After the outbreak of war, the Swiss decided to keep honoring those agreements, even though the Axis Powers were in control of most of those European countries at the time. That meant that Switzerland kept doing business with both the Allies and the Axis Powers.

During the war, Switzerland was pressured by both the Allies and the Axis Powers *not* to do business with the other side. If Switzerland gave in to one of those demands, but not the other, they would risk their neutrality. If they refused both, they would either starve or freeze, as they needed to import a lot of their food and nearly all of their fuel. So, to most people it was clear.

They had to keep doing business with both sides, even if it meant doing business with some very bad people

Likewise, the Swiss also chose to allow both the Allies and the Axis Powers to move people, food, and supplies through Switzerland, when needed. Switzerland, being located smack in the center of Europe, had to decide whether foreign trains could pass through, what they were allowed to carry, and how much of it.

When the other European countries fell under the control of the Axis Powers, their own currencies became worthless. Likewise, nobody else wanted to accept the currencies of the Axis Powers for international business deals. That meant that—for a while—the Swiss franc was the only major currency that could be freely used in Europe...and both the Allies and the Axis powers needed it. Both sides ended-up selling tons of gold to Switzerland in exchange for Swiss francs, which they then used to buy materials that were important to have during wartime—namely tungsten (a kind of mineral for hardening steel, which you need for weapons) and oil.

Here's the problem. The gold that Germany sold to Switzerland (about 1.2 billion Swiss francs worth of it) was mostly gold that the Germans had looted from the central banks of the other European countries they had invaded. It's not clear when Switzerland learned about that fact.

It gets worse.

Some of the gold Germany sold to the Swiss (at least 581,000 Swiss francs worth) was gold that had been stolen from Jewish victims sent to die in Nazi concentration camps.

Just when you thought it couldn't get any worse...think again.

Before and during the war, many Jews—afraid for their lives—put their valuables (such as gold, money, paintings, jewelry, etc.) in Swiss bank accounts for "safekeeping." After these people disappeared during the war, the Swiss banks kept these items for decades without trying very hard to find their rightful owners. When family members contacted the banks to collect the items, they were turned away, as their names weren't on the bank accounts.

The banks finally cooperated in the 1990s—fifty years later—
but only after a huge amount of pressure
was put on them from governments all over the world

The Swiss banks were able to hold out for so long because of bank secrecy, which meant that bankers are not allowed to reveal information about the people who hold accounts at their bank, or how much money is in a given account. This is great for people who want to hide money—particularly for bad people who want to hide money and don't want questions asked. By the end of World War I, Switzerland had become Europe's bank. The French deposited their money in Geneva, the Italians in Lugano, and the Germans in Zurich. In fact, at the start of World War II, even Adolf Hitler had an account with UBS (Union Bank of Switzerland) where he hid away the money he had made selling his book *Mein Kampf.*

Hitler never got to make a final withdrawal

Aftermath

During the years of World War II, the Swiss knew that they were no match for the German War Machine. They had to make a lot of really difficult decisions that:

1. kept the Germans from invading
2. kept the Swiss population alive and free
3. and, most importantly, kept one single safe haven—
one beacon of independence and democracy—
in a Europe that had become dark and terrifying

The Swiss, surrounded as they were by war and destruction, were able to manage that, against all odds, which is a miracle. But there is no doubt that Swiss action and inaction led to people's deaths and perhaps to the prolongation of the war. Many Swiss have accepted their fault. As Federal President Kaspar Villiger delared in 1995, "We made a wrong decision. The Federal Council deeply regrets this, and apologizes for it, in the full knowledge that such a failure is ultimately inexcusable." Stories have also come forward since that time about Swiss people who fought against Nazi Germany in quiet ways. Here are just a few.

Carl Lutz was a Swiss diplomat serving in Hungary who was given permission to issue letters of protection for 8000 Jewish people. Instead, he issued letters of protection for—and saved the lives of—approximately 62,000 Hungarian Jews.

Elsbeth Kasser was a nurse who spent her entire career helping children afflicted by war and improving the lives of people living in internment camps during World War II. During the war, she helped children at risk in France to cross the border to Switzerland.

Paul Grüninger was a police commander in St. Gallen at the border of Germany and Austria. When Hitler seized Austria, Jews rushed to get out. Grüninger understood and set about changing the dates on their visas and forging documents so they could get into Switzerland.

Recha Sternbuch was a woman from Montreux who saved thousands of Jewish refugees by smuggling them across the borders into Switzerland. She also helped to convince Jean Marie Musy, the former Swiss president and acquaintance of Hitler's #2 guy (Himmler), to negotiate the release of Jews from death camps in exchange for money.

Awesome

Johanna Spyri

Marie Heim-Vögtlin

Isabelle Eberhardt

Iris von Roten

A few amazing Swiss women

Women

Ruth Dreifuss

Martina Hingis

Guilia Steingruber

Helvetia

History books are full of tales of men doing great things. Meanwhile, quietly, in the background, women have been doing equally amazing things and not getting a fraction of the attention. Each of the following women is awesome in her own way and her story deserves to be told.

9th to 10th century: Saint Wiborada

Wiborada and her brother, Hatto, were born to a wealthy family in Klingnau, Aargau, sometime towards the end of the 9th century. Both Wiborada and Hatto forgave their parents for giving them such unusual names, but both ended up rejecting their family's privileged lifestyle.

The youngsters were known to forego parties in favor of inviting the sick and poor into the family home to recuperate

WIBORADA

Hatto was the first to leave home, becoming a monk at the Abbey of St. Gallen. When their parents died, Wiborada joined him at the Abbey. She made Hatto's clothes and helped to bind many books in the monastery library.

Wiborada and Hatto were very close...and rumors circulated that they were *too* close. Wiborada had to prove her innocence by undergoing "ordeal by fire." If you've never heard of this before, it's a *lot* less fun than it sounds.

Tips and tricks for holding your own successful Ordeal By Fire

Step 1: Heat ploughshares in fire...

Step 2: ...until they're red-hot.

Step 3: Cover ears while accused walks across them.

Step 4: See if the accused has
burned feet.

Step 4a: If feet are burned, call the
executioner. The accused is clearly guilty.

Step 4b: If feet are not burned,
the accused is innocent. Darn it.
Set them free.

Step 5: Grab next accused, reheat,
and repeat.

Wiborada either danced fast enough over the ploughshare or was truly innocent, as she made it across the red-hot ploughshare without frying her feet off. She was set free.

Hatto—being a man and all—was found to be innocent, and didn't have to risk singeing his ten little tootsies.

After that, Wiborada decided it was time to leave the abbey (and the ploughshares) behind, so she moved around to a couple of other churches before settling at the church of St. Magnus, also in St. Gallen.

Wiborada quickly got a reputation within the church for:

being very reclusive, praying in her room night and day when she wasn't sewing or binding books

being able to heal the sick and injured

having the gift of prophecy (that meant that she had visions of the future)

Those days, most people who said they had visions and could perform miracles were dismissed as crazy, but not Wiborada. She had tons of visitors and a set of devoted fans. In 925, Wiborada predicted a Hungarian invasion in St. Gallen and was also convinced that she would become a martyr (a.k.a., die) as a result. Upon hearing her prophecy, the monks hid the precious monastery books and wine, and then hid themselves in the nearby hills. Wiborada however, staying true to her destiny, refused to leave her chamber. Sure enough, there was a Hungarian invasion in 926.

The invaders broke through the roof of Wiborada's chamber and used a shepherd's axe to chop her head in half, proving her prophecy to be correct

In 1047, Pope Clement II formally declared Wiborada to be a saint—the first female saint in history. She is known as the patron saint of libraries and librarians and is most commonly shown in artwork holding a book and a halberd (which, by the way, is NOT the type of axe that was used to chop her skull in half). However, the halberd was not even invented until about 400 years after Wiborada's death.

1645–1714: Katharina von Wattenwyl

Then there was Katharina von Wattenwyl. Nobody quite knew what to make of this totally awesome woman.

Katharina von Wattenwyl was born into an aristocratic family, the youngest of eleven children. She grew up at Oron Castle in Vaud, where her father was the regional governor.

From a very young age, Katharina preferred horseback riding to handicrafts and was more interested in pistols than in playing with dolls

Katharina's parents had both died by the time she reached the age of thirteen (purely coincidental…nothing to do with Katharina's love of pistols). She was then passed off from relative to relative, none of them quite sure how to handle such a strong-willed young girl.

At the age of twenty, Katharina was involved in an argument with a lady of the French court and ended-up challenging her to a duel—with pistols—on horseback. Katharina's specialty. Once her family found out about the challenge, they arranged for the ammunition to be secretly removed from the pistols.

*Once Katharina realized what they had done,
the duel progressed into a swordfight until her family
put a stop to it yet again*

Another incident found Katharina taming a horse that had been labeled as untamable by every man who had tried to ride it. Katharina managed to tame the horse and ride it back to its owner. He was so appreciative that he gave her a set of pistols as a gift. Katharina found an excuse to use one of them soon after when a German count bothered her one day in the woods. She lost no time shooting him in the shoulder.

Katharina wasn't done. She had her portrait painted, but not the way a woman should.

If all that wasn't enough, Katharina then started spying for Louis XIV, "The Sun King" of France. It's not clear why she got involved in spying for the French king, but when one of her secret messages to the French Ambassador was intercepted, she was arrested and tortured until her trial. It was concluded that Katharina had accepted large sums of money for information she gave to the French about the Swiss intention to form an alliance with the British…most of which she made up. Katharina was sentenced to death, but even this she managed to get out of with the help of her family.

Afterwards, Katharina moved to Valangin Castle in Neuchatel, where she wrote her memoirs for King Louis XIV before her death. How else could we get such a fascinating peek into this extraordinary woman's life?

She posed as a warrior, with her long hair free and flowing, a chest plate of armor, and an ermine cape

1853–1901: Emilie Kempin-Spyri

Emilie's claim to fame, until fairly recently, was that she was the niece of Johanna Spyri—the woman who wrote *Heidi*. But Emilie Kempin-Spyri was so much more than just that.

Emilie Spyri was born the youngest of eight children and married a pastor, Walter Kempin, at the age of twenty-three. At first, everything about Emilie's life appeared quite normal.

What nobody (except Walter) knew was that Emilie had many more ambitions for her life. Eight years after marrying—and three children later—Emilie enrolled in Law School at the University of Zurich. Four years later, she finished her doctoral degree, graduating near the top of her class and becoming the first woman in Switzerland to graduate with a law degree. Great! So it was time to start being a lawyer, right?

Wrong.

In other words...Emilie was allowed to complete her law studies, but was not allowed to practice law. No girls allowed in the Boy's Club!

Emilie appealed to the Supreme Court—which also consisted of only men. They rejected her appeal. But Emilie pressed on, applying for the position of lecturer at the University of Zurich.

Many people didn't like that Emilie was trying to have a legal career, so they stopped coming to her husband's church. Emilie and Walter decided to try their luck elsewhere, and moved to New York City in 1889. It was here that Emilie flourished. She found teaching roles, published law papers, published books, and still found the time to start the Emily Kempin Law School AND take care of her family. But the family missed Switzerland, so they returned to Zurich, where Emilie was still not allowed to work as a lawyer. In 1891, she received an "exceptional" permission to teach at the University of Bern—meaning that, despite being a woman and not really being a valid lecturer, she was allowed to teach certain classes—of course being paid less than her male counterparts.

Emilie moved alone to Berlin to teach law for very little money. By 1897, after years of hard work, low pay, and ruined high hopes, an exhausted Emilie broke down. She was put into an insane asylum and given a string of cruel treatments, which only made her worse. She died in 1901 at the age of 48, just after a new law allowed women to practice law. Too late for Emilie Kempin-Spyri. But it never would have happened at all without Emilie's spirited fight for her own rights. Today, Emilie Kempin-Spyri is recognized as one of Europe's first female attorneys and as the first female university lecturer in Switzerland.

1917–2017: *Marthe Gosteli*

Marthe Gosteli was trained from a very young age to fight for what she believed in. Born to a simple farming family in Worblaufen, Bern, she watched her father take an active part in politics, while her mother sat on the sidelines.

Back then, Swiss women were not allowed to be involved in politics and did not even have the right to vote

Marthe was 40 years old when her father died, which left Marthe, her mother, and her sister in charge of the family farm... not so simple in a Man's World. Marthe had a friend (yes, a man) who helped her mother keep the farm. Without him, they surely would have lost it.

Marthe had seen enough. She joined the feminist movement in 1940 and decided to (1) earn her own money, (2) never get married, and (3) never have children.

Instead, she devoted herself 100% to the fight for women's equal rights

By 1964, Marthe was President of the Women's Suffrage Association in Bern, where she was trying to get women the right to vote. She wrote pamphlets and went door-to-door to discuss women's equal rights with anyone who would listen. She wanted to promote equality by convincing women to become more in-volved in their own communities.

In 1967, she was made Vice President of the Federation of Swiss Women's Associations. On February 7th, 1971, a majority of the voting men in Switzerland agreed that women should indeed have the right to vote on the national level. Switzerland was one of the last countries in Europe to grant women the right to vote. But it was done. Gosteli celebrated this victory, and then immediately got busy again.

Between 1970 and 1972, all Swiss cantons, except two,
agreed to grant women the right to vote.
The government finally forced Appenzell Ausserrhoden
and Innerrhoden to let women vote in 1989 and 1990.

She established the Gosteli Foundation in 1982 to preserve the history of Swiss women and their struggle for equality. It's grown into an extensive library, housed in Gosteli's childhood home that she fought so hard to protect all those years ago.

Gosteli died in 2017 at the age of ninety-nine, but not before receiving an honorary doctorate from the University of Bern and the Swiss Human Rights Award in 2011.

So, if you are a Swiss female and you are old enough to vote, remember Marthe Gosteli, get your bottom over to the polling place four times per year, and let your vote be counted. Marthe dedicated her entire life so you would have the right to do just that.

There-are-too-many-to-mention-but-here-are-some-more-awesome-Swiss-women

Johanna Spyri (1827–1901) was the aunt of Emilie Kempin-Spyri and one heck of an author. Born in Hirzel, near Zurich, she published dozens of books in her lifetime, including the world-famous *Heidi*, which Spyri wrote in only four weeks.

Marie Heim-Vögtlin (1845–1916) was born in Aargau and knew from a young age that she wanted to study medicine. She applied for admission to the University of Zurich and graduated with honors, becoming the first female physician in Switzerland in 1874. She quickly got a reputation as a talented doctor and went on to found Switzerland's first women's hospital and nursing school.

Isabelle Eberhardt (1877–1904) was born in Geneva in 1877 and educated at home by her father. Insanely intelligent, she spoke seven languages fluently before she was twenty. She was fascinated by Africa and wrote and published stories set there with remarkable detail, even though she hadn't traveled there yet. Eberhardt moved to Algeria in her twenties, often dressing as an Arab man, as she enjoyed the freedom it brought her. She even gave herself the male name of *Si Mahmoud Saadi* and continued to write, dress, and act as a man. She continued to write—most of her books were about unspeakable topics that shocked "good" society. The books of course didn't sell well, but Isabelle kept writing them anyway. She lived a wild, dangerous, unconventional life, which—for a woman at that time—was unheard of. Smoking, drinking, and drugs took their toll on her health. By the time she was twenty-seven, she had no money left, had lost all of her teeth, and was suffering from multiple diseases. She died that year in a flash flood in Algeria; books published after her death sold well and she finally made a name for herself in "good" society.

Iris von Roten (1917–1990) was unusual for a woman in the early 20th century. Well-educated and very outspoken, she worked as the editor of a women's magazine, as a lawyer, and was the author of a highly scandalous book titled *Women in the Playpen*. Her book criticized women's lack of power in society and attacked the domination of men. Switzerland wasn't quite ready for von Roten, though. Her book got really bad reviews from men and women alike, and a lot of anger was directed at her. So in 1960 she turned her back on the feminist movement, packed up her car, and drove by herself to visit Turkey, Iran, Iraq, Syria, Lebanon, Morocco, Tunisia, Sri Lanka, Brazil, and many places in between. A woman traveling these places alone was unheard of at that time, but von Roten had a blast.

Ruth Dreifuss (1940–) was born in St. Gallen, educated in Geneva, and worked in a variety of Swiss agencies and unions until her election to the Swiss Federal Council in 1993. Fluent in five languages, she served as President of the Swiss Federal Council in 1999, the first woman to ever be elected to that position. Not bad when you consider that women weren't even allowed to vote in national elections until 1971! As Minister of Home Affairs, Dreifuss pushed for a new law that would guarantee universal health care for the entire Swiss population. She is also a member of the Council of Women World Leaders, which concentrates on mobilizing female leaders worldwide to act on issues that are critical for women.

Martina Hingis (1980–) was born in Czechoslovakia and moved to Switzerland with her mother when she was seven years old. She started playing tennis when she was two, entered a tennis tournament when she was four, and at twelve was the youngest to ever win the girls' singles Grand Slam junior title at the French Open. Between the ages of fourteen and seventeen, Hingis climbed from world's 87th best to the undisputed best women's tennis player in the world. She continued to dominate women's tennis until her retirement in 2003. Unable to give up the game, she returned to tennis, only to retire once again in 2007 and 2017.

Guilia Steingruber (1994–) from St. Gallen is a Swiss artistic gymnast with an impressive record of "firsts." She is the first Swiss female gymnast to win the European all-around title and the first female Swiss gymnast to ever win a medal at the Olympics. She won a bronze medal on the vault at the 2016 Olympics, just a fraction of a point behind the silver and gold medal winners.

Helvetia (1848–) is the female national personification of Switzerland. Her name comes from the Latin name of Switzerland—Confœderatio Helvetica—and she is most often shown wearing a flowing gown, carrying a long spear, and holding a shield emblazoned with the Swiss crest. Clearly feminine, she's also a warrior, a defender, and a symbol of independence for the Swiss. You can see her on coins, postage stamps, and on many, many items in the tourist shops...

Criminal

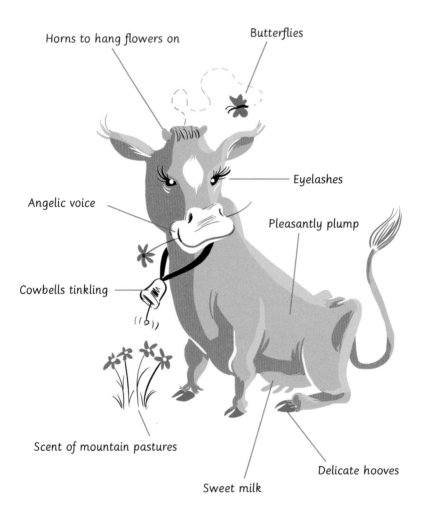

Horns to hang flowers on

Butterflies

Eyelashes

Angelic voice

Pleasantly plump

Cowbells tinkling

Scent of mountain pastures

Sweet milk

Delicate hooves

Our idea of Swiss cows

Cows

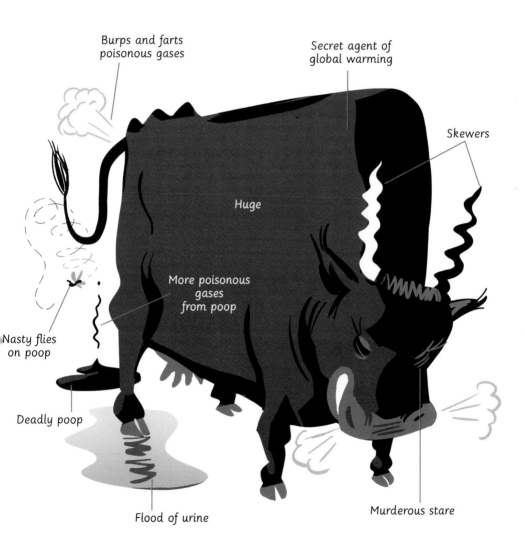

Burps and farts poisonous gases

Secret agent of global warming

Skewers

Huge

More poisonous gases from poop

Nasty flies on poop

Deadly poop

Flood of urine

Murderous stare

A real Swiss cow

They'll bat their long, luxurious eyelashes, showing off their big, brown, manipulative eyes. Those chocolaty eyes watch you—study you—as you walk past. *Tinkle, tinkle, tinkle* go their cowbells. But don't let them fool you. Not for a second.

If you've ever seen the Battle of the Queens, you have an idea of the power of the Swiss cow. If you haven't, you're really missing something.

The Cow Fights take place in the Valais region each spring, with 10–12 cows let loose in an arena at one time. Each cow picks her opponent and the two cows lock horns, testing each other's strength. The cows remain, head-to-head, horn-to-horn, pushing each other backwards, until one of them turns to run away. That cow not only loses the battle, but also takes the chance of getting the winner's horn tip stuck up her backside. The winning cow advances to the next round until the ultimate winner is crowned "Queen of the Queens."

No bull. Can you imagine if human monarchies worked things out this way?

Did you know that, worldwide, cows kill more people per year than sharks? No joke. Sharks chomp about seven people each year, compared to an average of twenty people obliterated by cows. Yet nobody has made a horror movie about a cow (but wouldn't *that* be cool?).

Alright, there are some good things cows do for us, and don't say we aren't thankful.

Cows...

...give us milk to drink and meat to eat.
...mow the grass of alpine pastures.
...keep farming a part of Swiss mountain culture (and those farms look cool).
...give us something to moo at during really boring car rides.

So, what are the cows' murderous methods? Let's start with their heads and move tailward, shall we?

Horns (a.k.a. the skewering tools)
Why do cows have cowbells?

Because their horns don't work.

But really, why do cows have horns? What purpose do they serve? More than most people realize.

Status symbol
Cows are social animals. They live in herds and each individual cow has its place within the group. Generally, the cows with the biggest, longest horns have higher status in the herd.

Grooming
Yep, cows use their horns to groom both themselves and other cows. Horn tips are very useful when a cow needs a good scratch in a particular place. If they can't reach the tickling place with their own horns, they'll use the tip of another cow's horns. They'll even use the tip of a buddy's horn to clean gunk out of their eyes. No joke. Each cow is totally aware of the size and curve of their horns and those of their friends. So, they know exactly how and where to scratch to get what they need. Get outside and watch some cows for a while if you don't believe me! Just don't expect them to scratch any of your own itchies...

Protection
Here's where the skewering comes in. What can a cow do if somone or something is threatening it, its calf, or its herd?
→ Pull out a sword?
→ Adopt a ninja warrior pose?
→ Be ready with a really nasty insult?

Nope. Cow horns are there to do serious damage to anything or anybody that angers, frightens, or otherwise irritates the cow. So maybe don't tell a cow any stupid cowbell jokes like the one above...

In 2017, a fifty-four year old woman was walking her dog in Chevenez, Jura, when she decided to cut across a fenced field full of 200 cows. Once she crossed the fence, she never had a chance. The cows charged, leaving her with three broken vertebra and eight broken ribs. They spared her life, though. Luckily for her, that particular herd of cows had been dehorned. So, no skewering... just a bit of squashing.

Ueli felt like he'd been up that tree for ages

Torso (a.k.a. the crusher)

The average cow weighs 753 kg and can run 35 km per hour. The average adult Swiss person weighs 70 kg and can run 40 km per hour. So, if both cow and human are on their feet, the human clearly has a slight advantage, right?

Even though they are really bulky, the cow (being a master of deception) can move a *lot* quicker than the average human reckons. Using this element of surprise, the cows' technique is to

233

knock the humans off their feet and then get busy crushing said human. If said human is particularly unlucky, they'll get skewered (see above) and trampled (see below), as well. Ouch.

In 2012, two women and a dog were hiking through an open pasture in Saint Gingolph, Valais, when they were attacked by a herd of cows. The cows managed to knock one of the women over and bonked her on the head. Apparently, it was only a warning, as they let her live to spread the tale amongst other humans who might dare enter the same pasture.

Let's not even get started on bulls, which, at 900 kg on average, weigh even more than cows. Granted, they run a bit slower than cows, but they are even more deadly than their "cow-nterparts." If they're angry and they manage to catch you, you're dead meat!

Legs and hooves (a.k.a. stampede specialties)

Cows and bulls can be highly unpredictable and—if somebody acts or reacts in the wrong way, or even spooks one cow—chances are high that they're going to get crunched up by the herd.

Herd attacks can be highly coordinated and designed to kill. When a herd feels defensive, the cows will gather in a circle. They will lower their heads and stamp the ground to scare off whatever is freaking them out. If that doesn't work, the higher-ranking cows will signal that the entire herd should stampede. They usually aim to first kick, butt, or shove the intruder...anything to knock them down to the ground. Then they get their heads beneath the victim, throwing them into the air and letting them crash back down to the ground—time after time after time. After time. Then comes the obligatory trampling.

In 2015, a German hiker was crossing an open pasture of cows with their calves in Laax. This hiker wasn't so lucky...the herd freaked out, knocked her over, and trampled her to death. No messing around with a mother cow!

Cows devising their evil plans

A: Human does something stupid and cow gets annoyed.	B: Cow catches human unaware.	C: Cow knocks human off feet.	D: Cow crushes human.	E: Cow skewers human, if desired.

Folks don't realize that most cow attacks are deliberate. That means that the cows *want* to hurt the people for whatever reason. So pay close attention, or risk finding yourself on the "business end" of an angry cow...or herd of cows!

The butt (a.k.a. the manure machine)

Yep. You read that right. Cow doo-doo is responsible for dozens of deaths in Switzerland per year. That's crappy, you say! Yes, exactly.

During 2013 alone, there were sixty-one (61!) major manure-related "accidents" affecting people in Switzerland. "How can that possibly be?" you ask. Isn't it fairly easy to avoid cow poop on any given day?

Unless you live in the countryside or go hiking with any regularity in the Alps, cow manure is more of a punchline than an actual danger in your life. The smell of freshly spread manure might burn your nasal passages a bit, but it won't kill you. Right?

Well, WRONG.

Deadly poop

Of the sixty-one "poop accidents" we're talking about above, forty-four of them were caused by inhalation of manure gases. These weren't caused by the abundance of cow patties in your local meadow or alpine walking path, because "what happens in the meadow stays in the meadow." The meadow patties dry out fairly quickly in the fresh air and don't release enough gases to harm a fly. In fact, the flies love them, but that's another story...

It's the cow poop on farms that causes the problem, especially during winter. The farmers keep their cows in a stall during the cold months and let all the poop and pee collect in underground storage tanks. It sits in there all winter, fermenting like fine wine, until it can be sprayed onto the fields in the spring as fertilizer. It's this liquified manure that is the really dangerous stuff.

If the gases wafting out of the collection tanks don't already poison you, try your very best not to fall into one of these fermenting manure tanks. It happens, apparently. Of those 61 major accidents mentioned above, 11 of them were due to falls into the manure tanks. Seriously. Sadly, some of those who perished in the poop did not fall into the tanks themselves, but rather jumped in to save somebody else who had...and never made it back out again. Dung-erous stuff!

Newly-applied hazard symbols

An additional six major accidents involved methane explosions that happened when the gases in the manure tanks built up too much pressure and—

Poop-plosion.

The butt—part 2 (a.k.a. the ozone assassin)

Although cows will never manage to kill us all with their horns, torsos, legs, hooves, or poop, they do have two final methods at their disposal. Farting and burping. And this might be the worst of all: it might even obliterate the entire human race.

You've heard of greenhouse gases, right? These are the gases that trap heat in the atmosphere, causing the earth to heat up. If average temperatures on earth keep increasing as they are, polar ice will continue to melt, ocean levels will continue to rise, and there will be more catastrophic weather-related events, such as hurricanes, floods, droughts, fires, etc.

The major contributors to greenhouse gases are fossil fuel-burning vehicles, electricity production that comes from the burning of fossil fuels, industries that burn fossil fuels for energy, and people who heat their homes using fossil fuels. In case you're wondering, fossil fuels include coal, oil, and gas.

So, what does all this have to do with cow burps and farts? Cows don't run on coal, oil, or gas, right? Right. But they do produce a lot of the same gases when they belch or "let one fly."

The Swiss Federal Office for the Environment estimates that Swiss cattle belch, squirt, and fart out about 6.4% of the country's greenhouse gases. A whopping three quarters of this comes from cow burps—the rest comes out the back ends of the cows. Add to all that an additional 2.2% of Swiss greenhouse gases coming from decaying poop in pits or on the fields, and so criminal cows are responsible for nearly 9% of Swiss greenhouse gases.

Cow burps and farts vs. car exhaust

Swiss cars, on the other hand, produce about 20% of the country's greenhouse gases. So, cars are causing twice the damage as all the burping, farting, poop-squirting cows.

Now consider that there are WAY more cars than cows in Switzerland. Four times more, in fact. As of 2017, there were about 6,053,000 cars in the country, compared to only 1,544,612 cows. So, one cow and her farts are worse than one car and its exhaust.

Proof yet again that these cute, cud-chewing moo-moos are out to get us...one way or another!

Contract

Beats

Homework

Devices

Bed

BOSS

Shoes (250 Fr.)

Family

Modern child

Children

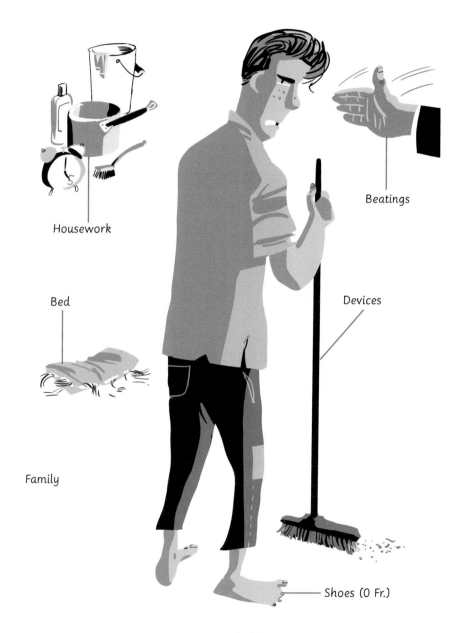

Housework

Beatings

Bed

Devices

Family

Shoes (0 Fr.)

Contract child

Here was what much of Europe looked like after World War I

In Switzerland, people were a bit better off. The Swiss had stayed out of World War I, but there were more poor, sick, and hungry people than ever. So, the Swiss government had an idea: it was time to "clean up" society. In their minds, *bad people* had *bad kids* and then those *bad kids* eventually made more *bad people*.

Who were the bad people who shouldn't have kids?

The very poor

The Very Poor were not hard to find. The authorities just had to look around the cities and villages. If they were in doubt, there were always neighbors willing to point judgmental fingers in the right directions.

The unmarried mothers

Look at all the women who had children without being married or had children and then somehow lost their husbands. Clearly a threat to society.

The Travelers

There were three different groups of "traveling people" in Switzerland and other countries in Europe—the Roma, the Senti, and the Jenish (or Yenish). They first arrived about 200 years ago and lived a nomadic lifestyle—traveling from place to place to work and live. It didn't take long for the "normal folks" with permanent homes in Switzerland to decide that the Travelers weren't to be trusted.

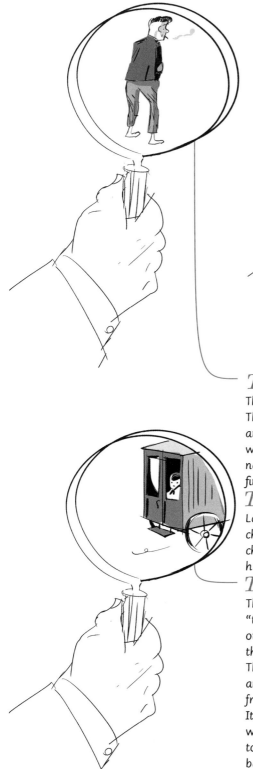

So, when your country is full of "bad people," such as those listed above, what should be done?

1. Help them?
2. Ignore them?
3. Take away their children so they slowly but surely disappear?

Well, the Swiss authorities chose Number 3. Between the 1920s and the 1980s, they took an estimated 100,000 undesirable children away from their undesirable families. The children were sent away to "normalize" their lives and cleanse them of their undesirable status.

So, how is that accomplished? The kids were forced to work under miserable conditions and never got paid for their efforts. Most people would call that *child slavery* but Switzerland chose to call them "contract children" instead.

Where were the ~~slaves~~ contract children sent to work?

1. Farm labor auctions: Yep, the authorities offered many of the children up for auction, sending them to the farming family that would accept the least amount of money from the government per month to care for the kid. Some of the children were then forced to work on the farms for twelve hours per day. Many had to sleep in the barn with the animals and were not allowed to eat with their contract families. They were often starved and abused. In the 1930s, one out of five people working on farms in canton Bern was under the age of fifteen. Most of those were contract children.

2. Foster care: There were some good foster families, of course. But most were just plain awful, with children being beaten, starved, abused, and also made to work long hours for no pay.

3. Institutions: If the kids were not able to work on a farm and were not accepted by foster families, they were stuck into retirement homes, insane asylums, or any other institution that had space for them. And then

they were made to work…even those that were barely old enough to walk.

4. Prisons: Some kids were simply put into jail, without having committed a crime or ever seeing the inside of a courtroom. Those kids got to work at the prisons, too.

So, to sum up, here were the options

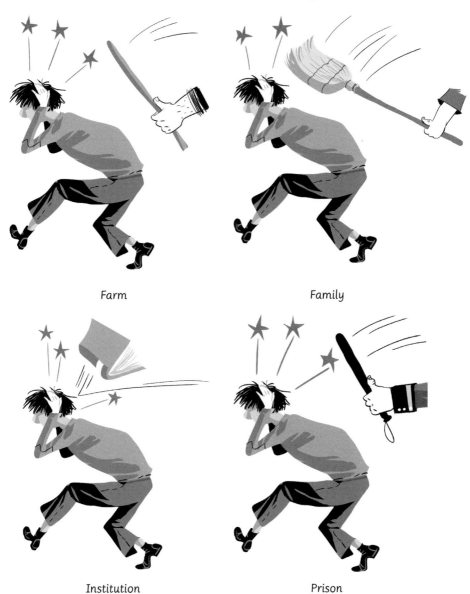

Farm

Family

Institution

Prison

Their parents were not given a choice in the matter. If they simply accepted their fate, they lost their children. If they put up a fight, they lost their children...but then they also faced the likelihood that they themselves would be thrown into an institution.

It was particularly bad for the Travelers. Many of these people not only had their children taken away, but soon afterwards found themselves forced to have sterilization surgery so they couldn't make any more Traveler children. Some of their children were also forced to have the same surgery to ensure that, when they got older, they wouldn't be able to make more Traveler children, either.

To add insult to injury, many of the parents had to pay money to the government every month to "take care" of their stolen and enslaved children.

Flash forward to the early 2000s. The practice of seizing children from "bad" families was long over, but the horrible memories for the surviving contract children and their families remained. Although most people in Switzerland knew what had happened, not many people were ready to talk about it. It took years and years, but shame and silence turned into whispers. Whispers turned into discussions. Grown-up contract children led the charge. They spoke up and spoke out. They gave interviews for magazines and on TV. They marched across Switzerland to raise awareness and to regain their honor. Finally, the government invited all surviving victims—both children and parents—to attend a ceremony in Bern where they were given a meal and a big, fat apology.

But a meal and a "sorry" simply were not enough.

In 2014, one of the former contract children launched a popular initiative. Before it came to a vote, the government acted and set aside 300 million Swiss francs for the surviving contract children and other people who were mistreated. The first ex-contract children started getting payments for their stolen childhoods in 2018.

So, the bottom line is…
- No child should ever be forced into slavery.
- No child should ever be forced into slavery.
- (oh, yes, just in case we forgot to mention…)

NO CHILD SHOULD EVER BE FORCED INTO SLAVERY

Awesome

The world with important Swiss inventions

Inventions

The world without important Swiss inventions

1659: Division symbol

You probably wouldn't consider the inventor of the division symbol to be very awesome...would you? After all, he's personally responsible for you having to do division in school, right?

But you'd be wrong. Johann Heinrich Rahn (1622–1676) was indeed awesome. By the time he was born in Zurich, people had been doing math—yes, including division—for many thousands of years. The Egyptians had it mostly figured out, but their methods weren't very exact.

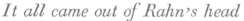

It all came out of Rahn's head

In 1659, Rahn invented the symbol, which is supposed to show the top number (represented by a dot) divided by the bottom number (also shown as a dot). Rahn's ÷ symbol caught on quickly in the US and Britain, but the rest of Europe didn't fall in love with it. The biggest problem was the fact that, back then, when ÷ was printed, it would take up three whole lines of space on the page. Printing in the 1600s was not as advanced as it is today, so this was a huge problem. A German mathematician tried to simplify things and save space by changing the ÷ symbol to : in 1684. The : symbol is still used throughout most of Europe today. The Americans and the British are still hooked on Rahn's ÷ symbol. So, I guess you could say that people are still pretty divided on the issue.

1819: Chocolate bars

People have been enjoying chocolate since about 350 BC, long before there was anything known as "Swiss chocolate." Cacao trees grow naturally in Central America, and the Mayan people there smashed the cacao bean into a paste and mixed it with chili peppers, cornmeal, and water to make a chocolaty drink. It was bitter and gritty but loved by Mayans and Aztecs alike.

Mayan dentists had their hands full back then

Cacao first came to Europe after Christopher Columbus hauled a bunch of cacao beans from Central America back to the Spanish royal family in the early 1500s…who went royally nuts over them! They added sugar and honey to the cacao drink, so it was sweeter, but still gritty and crunchy. It also made the expensive drink even more expensive, as sugar was not easy to come by in those days.

Missing teeth and massive cavities were all the rage,
once the royals had them

Once the rest of Europe found out about cacao beans, the race was on to make the best drinking chocolate. Until the early 1800s, chocolate remained a drink for the wealthy. Then along came Francois-Louis Cailler (1796-1852) from Vevey, Switzerland. Chocolate—and how it was consumed—changed forever.

Cailler got his first taste of Italian chocolate at a local fair when he was a teenager. He loved it so much, he decided to go to Italy to study chocolate-making. When he returned to Switzerland, he brought his new knowledge with him (which didn't exactly thrill the Italians), and set up his own chocolate factory in Vevey in 1819. At first, he sold his chocolate paste as a gritty—and super expensive—health tonic.

Over time, though, Cailler found a way to make a solid, smooth chocolate that could be formed into bars—and then he automated the process with machines. Suddenly it was much cheaper to produce his chocolate, which made it affordable for nearly everyone. Now we can all have the pleasure of holding the solid chocolate he invented in our hands—and letting it melt all over our fingers. Who doesn't love licking that smooth, creamy sticky stuff off their fingers?

1843: Sugar cubes

Up until 1843, people bought sugar in large, brown, cone-shaped lumps (ummm…sounds yummy, doesn't it?) and then chopped off what they needed when cooking or baking. Chopping the sugar to the right size was a tough job, especially considering that the only tools available at the time were heavy, cast-iron, finger-pinching tongs and nippers.

Close-up of finger-pinchers

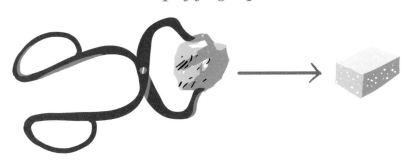

Jakob Christof Rad (1799-1871) from Rheinfelden, Switzerland, was the director of a beet sugar refinery. He and his wife, Juliana, had sixteen (yes, sixteen!) children, so you've already guessed that Juliana was chopping chunks off the big brown sugar lump pretty often. After nipping her fingers for the umpteenth time, she asked Jakob to find a way to make single-serve lumps of sugar. After some experimenting, Jakob invented a way to grate the huge lumps of sugar, dampen it just right, and then press it into little molds that would dry overnight. He presented his stump-fingered wife with a box of sugar cubes, which thrilled her (and their sixteen kids). Jakob then went on produce ten tons of sugar cubes per day, selling them all across Europe.

Sweet success!

1923: *the Riri zipper*

Martin Othmar Petrus Notker Winterhalter (1889-1961) was a totally normal guy...NOT. He was born in St. Gallen in 1889, the youngest of seven children. From the start, he was known as the crazy one...and his six siblings never let him forget it, calling him a variety of "crazy"-related names his entire life. Winterhalter proved their point by getting thrown out of a few schools and then, when he did manage to graduate, using up his entire inheritance on one insane trip through France. During that trip, Winterhalter got a taste for the good life and decided that he would be a millionaire—but he would achieve it on his own, not through inheritance. He started studying law in Germany in 1911, paying for his education by inventing a bandage that was very popular with older officers during World War I who had hernias (which is when you have a hole in your stomach muscle and your guts start spilling out).

It should have been called
The Winterhalter Hernia Holder

Soon after, an American visited Switzerland with a strange product—a zipper. Not just any zipper, but a horrifically complicated zipper that nobody in their right mind would ever use. It had hooks on either side of the zipper itself that had to be attached to eyes before the zipper could be pulled shut, taking ages to close.

*The inspiration for the **RiRi** zipper*

The local embroidery experts laughed at his ideas and sent him to the only person they knew who might be crazy enough to be interested—Martin Winterhalter.

Winterhalter was not only interested. He sold everything he and his wife owned, right down to their silverware, in order to buy the idea—which was probably about the same time his wife started thinking about leaving her crazy husband (which she eventually did). Winterhalter then spent the next few years redesigning the zipper, replacing the hooks and eyes with *ribs* and *grooves* (*Rippen* and *Rillen*). The *Riri* zipper was born in 1925. Then things really got crazy.

The Riri zipper made Winterhalter fabulously rich. By 1929, the Riri zipper was being produced in Luxembourg, Germany, Italy, and Switzerland, and was shipped all over the world. Business was booming.

But, as with many cases of fame and fortune, destruction and misfortune follow closely behind. At about the age of 40, Winterhalter hit his head while skiing in Engelberg. Soon after, he started doing a few even-crazier things that greatly alarmed his siblings:

1. he started talking about designing and creating buildings and roads that could be made of Riri zippers,

2. he became convinced that magical stones he found in his garden could help people in the afterlife, and

3. (perhaps the most troubling for his siblings) he started spending a LOT of his money on a string of very young, pretty secretaries.

Zipper zones

By 1941, it was clear to his siblings that Winterhalter was totally bonkers. It also occurred to them that Winterhalter did not have any children. This meant that there was no heir to inherit his massive zipper fortune. What would happen to all that money when he died? Hmmm?

It might, or might not, have been a coincidence that his siblings arranged for Winterhalter to be kidnapped from his home, drugged, thrown into a car, and transported to Burghölzli, the famous insane asylum in Zurich.

Zipped out

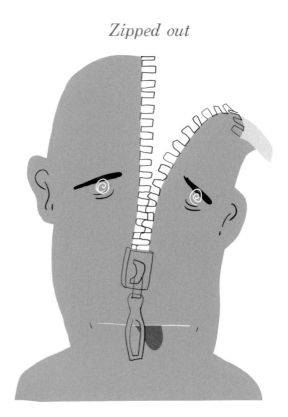

The doctor at Bürghölzli released Winterhalter after only a few days, but Winterhalter's siblings did not give up. They had him locked up in a string of other insane asylums, hoping one of them would finally keep him caged in for good. Winterhalter escaped from each and every asylum with the help of his string of very young, pretty secretaries, until his luck ran out. He was unable to break out of the last asylum, where he stayed locked up for eleven years...until he died.

Nobody knows what happened to Winterhalter's massive fortune. It's quite the secret...and the lips of his extended family are all zipped up, as well.

1951: *Velcro*

George de Mestral (1907–1990) was an electrical engineer from Vaud, Switzerland who'd had a flair for inventions from a very young age.

One day in 1941, de Mestral went hiking in the Jura mountains and came home to find seed pods stuck to his shoes, his clothes, and his dog. After looking at them through a microscope, he saw that the pods had tiny hooks on their coatings that made them stick to any surface that had an available loop for them to cling to.

Good dog

Bada-bing-bada-bam! An idea was born. For the next several years, de Mestral experimented with re-creating the hook and loop shapes on different types of materials...but none of them stuck.

Not ready to quit, de Mestral toured fabric manufacturing plants and told them about his idea. The first six companies laughed him out the door. Finally, he found a manufacturer who didn't think the idea was totally nuts. Together they combined cotton fabric with tough nylon...and it stuck.

A name was born—Velcro—which de Mestral invented using a combination of the French words for "velvet" and "crochet."

Great, so success, right?

De Mestral hoped Velcro could be used in the fashion industry as a more reliable, less frustrating version of the zipper, which was known to catch and break. But nobody wanted to use Velcro, as they said it looked like left-over bits of cheap fabric.

Velcro finally "stuck" after NASA saw the potential to use it in space flight. They stuck one side onto the interior walls of the spacecraft, and the other side onto the astronauts' tools.

Great! No tools floating away any more

Once Velcro had its great space debut on international television, it became popular for all kinds of things, including sports gear, wetsuits, scuba gear, jackets, office equipment, sporting goods, wallets, and—yes—Finally, clothing. In the 1960s, the fashion designer Pierre Cardin became obsessed with Velcro. Other designers caught onto the idea shortly thereafter. The world is now stuck with Velcro.

1939: Smell-O-Vision

The Swiss are known to be an innovative bunch who are excellent at finding or inventing original solutions to problems or questions. They've had their share of muck-ups, though. For example, Smell-O-Vision.

Hans Laube (1900-1976) believed that everything on earth, even emotions, has a scent. Too bad he didn't leave the idea right there. In Zurich in the 1930s, Hans came up with an idea for a device that would pump aromas into movie theaters to match what was going on in the movie itself.

So, if you were watching *The Sound of Music* when Maria dances on the hilltops, you would smell freshly cut grass. If you were watching *Twilight* when vampires are sucking on some poor soul's neck, you would smell blood. If you were watching *101 Dalmatians* squatting in the poop-filled dirt...well, you get the idea.

Hans presented Smell-O-Vision at the New York World's Fair in 1939, but it stink-bombed. Then he tried to sell the idea to TV and movie studios in Hollywood, but nobody quite caught the whiff of possibility.

Enter Hollywood producer and gimmick-lover Michael Todd. The two men teamed up to release a film in 1960 called *Scent of Mystery*. Bad idea. Technology being what it was back then... there were some problems.

Some people said the smells were too strong. Others said they were too weak. The people in the balcony didn't smell the smells until it was too late. Other people felt sick. There were hissing sounds when the scents were released from the pipes, and some people couldn't hear the movie as other people were sniffing too loudly.

Scent of Mystery was dubbed a "stinker" and disappeared as quickly as it had been released. In 2000 it landed on *Time Magazine*'s list of the Top 100 Worst Ideas of All Time. Poor Hans.

A few other notable Swiss inventions

1908: Toblerone

Mountain-shaped chocolate bar invented by the Tobler cousins in Bern in 1908. About 62,000 kilometers of Toblerone are eaten worldwide per year, which is longer than the circumference of the earth.

1912: Aluminum foil

Dr. Lubner, Neher & Cie started making aluminum foil in Emmishofen, Switzerland. Until then, tin foil had been used to wrap food, but it wasn't easy to bend around the food and left it with a lingering taste of tin. Yum. Using aluminum instead of tin solved both problems.

1938: Nescafé

When Brazilian coffee bean sales dropped in 1930, the Brazilian government asked Nestlé to develop a coffee that could be made by simply adding water. After seven years of research, Nestlé launched Nescafé on April 1st, 1938. Today, more than 5500 cups of Nescafé are consumed every second worldwide.

1952: Rivella

Rivella is considered the national drink of Switzerland. It has an unlikely success story, as it's a carbonated drink made of herbal and fruit extracts, sugar, and whey (a by-product of cheese production). Urp!

1981: Swatch watch

During the 1960s and 70s, cheap Japanese digital watches invaded the market and sales of traditional analog watches sank. The Swiss, known for high-quality, highly expensive timepieces, fought back with the cheap, trendy Swatch watch, and now lead markets in both cheap and expensive watches.

THE END

So. There you have it. That's Switzerland and its untold, bloody, and absolutely real history. I managed to avoid mentioning:

...cuckoo clocks (not even once!)
...Heidi (well, OK...once)
...chocolate (only a few times)
...and William Tell (OK, he got a whole chapter...but, yeah).

Now you know so much more about Switzerland's past—both the amazing and admirable parts and the not-so-amazing and less-than-admirable parts.

We are all part of Switzerland's present, which eventually will become history, as well. So this isn't really the end. What will Switzerland's future look like? Well, that's where we all come in.

Acknowledgements

Thanks to my intrepid critique partners, who have stuck by me
since the first glimmer of a book about Switzerland crossed
my mind. Joy Manné, Anita Lehmann, Jeannine Johnson Maia,
Katie Hayoz, and Monica Layton...I couldn't have pulled this
off without all of you.

Love and thanks to my parents, Chuck and Susan Delarue.
Two of the funniest people I know. Seriously.

Thanks to Dario Trinkler for all the research tips and sources,
as well as Corina Cahenzli for the Romansh, and Aline Jakob and
Fiona Rüegg for the Schwyzertüütsch.

Richard Harvell, thank you for believing I could actually do
this and then for standing by me while I did it.
My thanks and respect to Satu Binggeli and Melanie Beugger
at Bergli Books. We couldn't have done this without you.

Finally, Michael Meister, thank you for bringing it all to life.

–Laurie Theurer

It was not always easy to draw all those murdered,
abused, and tortured people who lead the way
through this book. It seems like Swiss history was not always
likable. Still, there are cool things like democracy
and chocolate. So, I hope that this book will help you bear
our history, and make it better for the future.

–Michael Meister